I0820081

Anna Stanford

Spinning plates

Easy Dinners with Simple Substitutions for Busy Families

This book is dedicated to Nigel, always my biggest supporter and chief taster. His passion for food made my job so much easier.

First published in Great Britain in 2025 by Hamlyn, an imprint of
Octopus Publishing Group Ltd
Carmelite House
50 Victoria Embankment
London EC4Y 0DZ
www.octopusbooks.co.uk
www.octopusbooksusa.com

An Hachette UK Company
www.hachette.co.uk

The authorized representative in the EEA is Hachette Ireland, 8 Castlecourt Centre, Dublin 15, D15 XTP3, Ireland (email: info@hbgi.ie)

Distributed in the US by Hachette Book Group
1290 Avenue of the Americas, 4th and 5th Floors
New York, NY 10104

Distributed in Canada by Canadian Manda Group
664 Annette St., Toronto, Ontario, Canada M6S 2C8

ISBN 978-0-600-63954-1
eISBN 978-0-600-63955-8

A CIP catalogue record for this book is available from the British Library.

Printed and bound in China.

10 9 8 7 6 5 4 3 2 1

Junior Commissioning Editor: Isabel Jessop
Editor: Scarlet Furness
Copy Editor: Anne Sheasby
Art Director: Yasia Williams
Photographer: Chris Terry
Food Stylist: Holly Cochrane
Food Stylist Assistants: Emma Cantlay & Caitlin Macdonald
Prop Stylist: Tamsin Weston
Production Manager: Caroline Alberti

Standard level spoon measurements are used in all recipes.
1 tablespoon = one 15ml spoon
1 teaspoon = one 5ml spoon

Both imperial and metric measurements have been given in all recipes. Use one set of measurements only and not a mixture of both.

Eggs should be medium unless otherwise stated. The Department of Health advises that eggs should not be consumed raw. This book contains dishes made with raw or lightly cooked eggs. It is prudent for more vulnerable people such as pregnant and nursing mothers, the elderly, babies and young children to avoid uncooked or lightly cooked dishes made with eggs. Once prepared these dishes should be kept refrigerated and used promptly.

Milk should be full fat unless otherwise stated.

Fresh herbs should be used unless otherwise stated. If unavailable use dried herbs as an alternative but halve the quantities stated.

Ovens should be preheated to the specific temperature.

Pepper should be freshly ground black pepper unless otherwise stated.

This book includes dishes made with nuts and nut derivatives. It is advisable for customers with known allergic reactions to nuts and nut derivatives and those who may be potentially vulnerable to these allergies, such as babies and children with a family history of allergies, to avoid dishes made with nuts and nut oils. It is also prudent to check the labels of pre-prepared ingredients for the possible inclusion of nut derivatives.

Vegetarians should look for the 'V' symbol on a cheese to ensure it is made with vegetarian rennet.

Contents

Foreword

Families evolve over time: they are ever-changing organisms, with differing needs, tastes and priorities. This won't be news to anyone, it's what we all sign up for and, if I'm honest, the resulting energy is the bit that I love most about family life. I am at my best when I am busy, and if you follow my Instagram page you will be aware that I've become an expert when it comes to finding ways to complicate my life. On top of three children, I just can't seem to say no to another pet... alpacas, you say? Yes please. Chickens? Why, of course! And just for good measure let's throw in a few cats and a couple of dogs. It may be hectic, but it's my idea of heaven.

This last year, however, has been something quite different. In December 2023, I lost my husband, following his long battle with prostate cancer. He was 58 years old and we had been married for 21 years. As a consummate planner, this wasn't something I had prepared for, and I was left feeling utterly rudderless as I aimed to forge a new normal for my family.

Needless to say, the time while Nigel was ill and the months following his passing were incredibly tough. In the early days, meals were delivered to our door by kind friends, but a life with teens and animals means that when the help inevitably stops, you must put one foot in front of the other and look to the future. I have learned this year that I can't carry everything for everyone, and I can't fix everything. However, eventually it must all continue and my second book – a long-term goal of mine – felt a strangely appropriate form of motivation. I wouldn't have felt myself if I didn't continue spinning plates.

My cookery has always given me a purpose alongside being a mum, and having something positive to channel my energy into was a vital distraction through hard times. Mealtimes, whether hurried or leisurely, have the power to ground us into our surroundings through a feeling of comfort and familiarity, and I appreciate more than ever the importance of simple, hearty staples to get the family together around the table. For all households, so many important conversations (and silent times) take place during family meals.

Whatever your evolving family currently looks like, I hope the recipes in this book go some way to helping make family mealtimes easy and enjoyable.

Welcome to *Spinning Plates*

Balancing the frequently conflicting demands of family life is a skill that no one ever teaches you. One moment you are in your twenties, blissfully spending an entire day preparing for a hedonistic dinner party with friends, then you look up and you're catering for five individuals with the patience of particularly grumpy hyenas and you still have laundry to do, work to complete and miles to drive to deliver them to various activities. Family life isn't a competitive game of Top Trumps, but a balancing act. Often it can feel like some of the plates we are spinning are fine bone china, some have minds of their own and some are on fire – the skill is to keep them all intact.

My family has again evolved. As I write this book my children are now aged 15, 17 and 20. Mia, my resident vegetarian, is now at university but comes home regularly. She will most likely move back home at the same time Tom goes to university. Thankfully I have our youngest, Finn, at home for at least three more years. The likely reality, in the current climate, is that they will all still be living at home when they're 30!

So, who is this book for? Everyone. I hope that every member of your family will find something that inspires them to cook. Whether you are accomplished in the kitchen or lacking confidence, a student or a parent looking to encourage children to get involved in mealtime preparation, there is something in here for you.

Cooking is a life skill, and is often overlooked in schools. It is so important that children grow up understanding food and without a fear to try new things and flavours. If we can encourage curiosity in our kitchens, we will have a whole new generation of competent cooks! Cooking is also a way to express yourself, and the more confident you feel about food, the more enjoyment you will get from it. So, take these recipes as a foundation and freestyle away. And if you don't have the confidence just yet, I have plenty of suggestions and tips for you!

Cook Clever

I'm not a purist when it comes to cooking, possibly due to my self-taught background, meaning I prefer to see recipes as guidelines rather than written in stone. I've never been scared to experiment, and in this endeavour I have frequently discovered new dishes and techniques, as well as improved flavours.

Adaptations

Many of my followers on social media share their frustrations with catering for a household with different nutritional requirements and the need for adaptation being forced on them. Every family will have members with an intolerance or a strong dislike of certain foods. This can prove challenging when trying to cater for everyone. My daughter Mia became vegetarian as a pre-teen and despite my love of cooking, initially I fell into the trap of making separate meals which was a time-consuming approach. To save my sanity, I learned to adapt my family's favourite recipes to work for us all. The same approach can be used to cater for different budgets and tastes.

This is where a strategically stocked store cupboard is key: with the right basics, you can use whatever fresh ingredients you have in your refrigerator to create endless options. The recipes in this book use accessible ingredients and equipment found in most people's cupboards. Most recipes have options for different cooking methods, such as the air fryer and slow cooker, as well as suggested ingredients swaps and tips to adapt for vegetarians, intolerances and allergies.

Organization & Meal Planning

I am always raving about meal planning. It doesn't need to be onerous, or mean you need to plan the whole week ahead (although for years with a young family I did). Instead, with the cost of catering for a household at the forefront of every home cook's mind, it drives us to be a little smarter when it comes to budgeting and minimizing food wastage.

Before you go to the supermarket, rummage through the refrigerator first, make a rough plan of what you intend to cook over the next few days, taking into consideration your family's commitments and activities. There's no point chucking some steaks into your shopping basket which need to be eaten in two days if you already have chicken in the refrigerator about to go past its use-by date. Stop and think if it is more practical in this situation to batch cook a one pot which can be stored in the refrigerator for a couple of days or be frozen into individual portions if it doesn't get eaten.

Freezer Top Tips

This leads me on to making the most of your freezer. It shouldn't be a dungeon of lost causes, but rather your waste-minimizing saviour. I firmly advocate you should avoid shopping for your freezer. Instead, use it as a way to maximize the life of items in the refrigerator or store cupboard. This means not losing sight of your meal plan when shopping and being lured into bulk-buying for the sake of it. There will always be items that you pick up from the frozen section: ice cream, peas, chips, out-of-season fruits and frozen spinach all have a well-earned place in my freezer. However, I avoid buying large packs of food to have in the freezer, just in case.

- There are some condiments that will go off when opened, even when left in the refrigerator, before you need to use them again. How many times have you opened a jar of pesto to find something unpleasant on the top? Pesto, tomato purée, garlic purée, pastes (such as harissa) and stock can all be frozen. Dollop on to nonstick baking paper, or into ice-cube trays, peel off/pop out and freeze in a labelled container or bag.
- All bread products can be frozen. In fact, there is a theory that bread which has been frozen is actually better for you, as the freezing process turns starch into resistant starch which is good for the gut.
- Check your vegetable drawer in the refrigerator. If there are vegetables that are going to go off and you don't have a use for them that day, freeze them. Blanch green veg such as broccoli and beans for a couple of minutes first. Freeze whole tomatoes, then plunge into boiling water straight from the freezer. Peel off their skins and use them for tomato pasta sauces or in place of canned chopped tomatoes.
- The same goes for fruit. Open-freeze berries on a baking tray and then decant into containers or freezer bags. If bananas are turning in the fruit bowl, pop them in the freezer whole in a container or freezer bag. They can be used straight from the freezer for smoothies or baking.
- How many times have you stumbled across a mystery dish in your freezer drawer? Label your freezer parcels with the contents and number of portions. You can use masking tape and a marker pen on plastic tubs or just use a marker pen on bags.
- When meal planning, do a freezer audit and incorporate it into your meal plan. If you keep it on your phone, you can refer to it when doing your food shop.

Batch Cooking

Prepping ahead, batch cooking and freezing are all such time savers and a habit that, once you have got into, you will find hard to reverse. I never, ever make Bolognese, chilli or a curry for two to four people. If you're going to the effort of buying ingredients, chopping veg, measuring out spices, browning meat and so on, why not get at least two meals out of it, if not more? Batch cooking and freezer meals offer flexibility for the busy family. Some evenings you will have a full house, on other evenings Jane will want her dinner when she gets back from football and Joe will want to eat the minute he comes home from school. When portioning meals, give yourself options for one, two or family servings.

Equipment Notes

There is a whole host of whizzy kitchen gadgetry out there and it is easy to fill your cupboards with redundant equipment that was bought on a whim. I am frequently asked for recommendations on what equipment I use and I find myself having to admit that I can often be found using bits handed down from my mum. So, I won't presume to tell you what you must have, but rather the list below includes all items that I use on repeat and that you will find useful for the recipes in this book.

Three Different-sized Lidded Saucepans

We all went Teflon mad and now there is massive pushback against this technology. Teflon has the advantage of being nonstick, but there's evidence to suggest that after frequent use it is harmful to us. Stainless-steel, ceramic or granite are the best non-toxic hardwearing pans.

A Large, Heavy-based Flameproof Lidded Casserole Dish

I find 26–28cm (10½–11 inch)/5–7 litre (8¾–12⅓ pint) capacity is ideal.
In America, this is known as a Dutch oven. Typically, the pans are cast iron, therefore heavy, which may not be for everyone, but they cook evenly and retain the heat so well, plus they can be used both on the hob and in the oven. I use mine all the time. It's worth getting a good-quality one, although I have been impressed with some of the supermarket copies of the high premium brands.

A Large, Heavy-based Nonstick Frying Pan

A 30cm (12 inch) diameter frying pan with at least an 8cm (3¼ inch) depth is so useful. Even more useful is when it is transferable from hob to oven. This means no plastic or wooden handles! The models with the removable handles are brilliant.

A Large, Nonstick Roasting Tray that Goes from Hob to Oven

If you find one with handles, even better! I use two sizes all the time. One is 27cm (10¾ inch) square and the other is 36 x 27cm (14¼ x 10¾ inches). Having a roasting tray that you can use on the hob and transfer to the oven saves on a lot of washing-up. You can brown meat or veg off first without the need to transfer to a different dish, or transfer the tray from the oven to the hob if you need to reduce sauces or make a gravy from the juices of a roast.

Measuring Spoons, Cups & Jugs

A set of good measuring spoons, cups and jugs for liquids are a must.

A Blender

This doesn't have to be a huge blender or food processor that takes up too much room on your worktop. My bullet and hand-held blenders get so much use when making pastes, smoothies and sauces.

Ovenproof, Freezerproof Dishes

These aren't as hard to source as they sound. When batch cooking big meals, putting extra portions in ceramic, metal or Pyrex (or similar suitable glass) dishes means these can go into the freezer and then be whipped out when needed, defrosted and put into the oven.

Wooden Chopping Boards

I am an avid collector of wooden chopping boards. Not only are they items of beauty, but wooden chopping boards are also a practical must. There are plenty of plastic alternatives, but these have been shown to degrade, with the danger of them releasing tiny plastic particles into your food over time. People worry about the hygiene of wooden chopping boards, but wood has natural antibacterial properties that inhibit bacterial growth. Clean with washing-up liquid and you can also treat with non-toxic antibacterial spray or wipe with half a lemon for a totally natural antibacterial treatment.

Pestle & Mortar

It doesn't get used daily but a heavy pestle and mortar is so useful for grinding small amounts of spices and pastes when you don't want to use a blender.

Colanders

One small and one large. You can't live without them in a family kitchen!

Knives

These are most certainly investment pieces. Buy well as they get used every single day and you will have them for years. I bought two good knives for my daughter to take to uni with her her: a paring knife – so versatile with a slim, sharp blade for slicing, skinning, chopping and peeling – and a humble bread knife. If you want to add to your collection, a utility knife, fillet knife and cleaver are all very useful. Sharpen them regularly (I'm terrible for this!).

Separating Jug

This is one of the simplest yet hardest working bits of kit in my kitchen. It's essentially a jug with a spout that pours from the bottom. Use it to separate the fat from stocks, sauces and gravies. Even better are the jugs which have a colander lid.

Cooking Options

Whether you are an air-fryer afficionado or a stalwart of the good old slow cooker, we have a multitude of ways to cook. To reflect this, where possible in the recipes, I have offered air-fryer and slow-cooker instructions to allow for whatever your preference may be.

Air Fryer

Air fryers are now so popular and regularly used in lots of family homes for very good reasons. They're cheaper to run than an oven, they tend to be much quicker and typically they are easy to clean. A ham or pork belly joint takes a fraction of the time in the air fryer than it does in the oven, making it a more achievable mealtime solution midweek. It's also a great tool for reheating certain foods – roast potatoes, Yorkshire puddings and pastries to name a few. It's also handy when I'm lacking oven space, or on busy mornings when I can pop bacon, sausages and even eggs into the basket, then run upstairs to get ready before throwing them on to a plate or into a sandwich.

I own a one-drawer model. I stewed over whether I should get a two-drawer one but personally I like the larger basket capacity of mine. If you are a smaller family or plan to use your air fryer in place of your oven, a larger two-drawer model might be the way forward, as long as you have the space to house it.

Where possible, I have provided instructions and timings for the use of an air fryer throughout this book. If the timings or guidelines aren't there, it's probably because it's not practical to use an air fryer, either because of the limitations of the capacity or the recipe is simply better cooked another way.

Tips for the air fryer:

- Buy either some paper or reusable liners. They are really handy to save washing the entire fryer each time you use it but also to hold juices, marinades and sauces.
- Make sure the air can circulate from the bottom up through the basket of the air fryer so that food cooks evenly.
- Preheat the air fryer (unless otherwise specified). Otherwise, you will need to add some cooking time to your recipes.

Slow Cooker

Not all slow cookers are equal, so it is always best to refer to the guidelines for your particular model, but these are my general tips to consider when using one.

Tips for the slow cooker:

- Brown meat first. You don't need to do this with minced meat or chicken, but larger cuts of red meat nearly always benefit from being seared first on the hob to seal in the flavour. In some cases, the slow cooker pan is compatible for cooking on the hob which saves on washing-up. Otherwise, sear meat first in a frying pan.
- I always colour onions and garlic in a little oil first, otherwise I have found that they can release a slightly bitter or metallic taste.
- Preheat the slow cooker (unless your model specifies otherwise). This will get food cooking straight away at a safe temperature.
- Slow cookers have their limitations – they will not brown meat or crisp skin or fat. If cooking a chicken with skin on or a joint of meat (such as pork) where the skin requires crisping, transfer the cooked joint to a lined baking tray and finish it in a hot oven.
- Most slow-cooker lids have a steam hole in the top. This is not only a safety feature but it allows sauces and stocks to reduce as they would in the oven at higher temperatures. Sometimes people report that stews, casseroles and curries are too liquid even after their long stint in the slow cooker. Slow cooker cooking is all about knowing your own model. If you find this to be the case, there are a few things you can do:

    - Reduce the amount of liquid you add to the recipe by 30%.
    - Leave the lid partly off for the last hour of the cooking process.
    - Turn the setting from low to high.
    - Strain off the sauce into a pan and simmer on the hob until reduced/thickened.
    - Transfer the dish to a conventional oven for a brief period (30 minutes or so) for the last stage of the cooking process.

Store-cupboard Essentials

If I were to impart one piece of advice to anyone reading this book, it would be to keep your store cupboard stocked up with strategic basics. It will be your best friend, and with those basics to hand you will have the building blocks to make any number of meals.

Actually, there's a second bit of advice coming your way – always read the labels. So many everyday products are full of nasties. We've all been aware of avoiding E-numbers and sugar for decades, but there's much evidence now to suggest that palm oil and trans fats increase bad cholesterol; stabilizers and emulsifiers negatively affect the gut's microbiome; and sodium nitrate and nitrate used as preservatives can form nitrosamines which are linked to cancer and can impact heart health. Take a can of coconut milk, for example – some are pure coconut and water, others have all sorts added to them. Many products are marketed as healthy – breakfast cereals, bread products and energy bars are particularly guilty of this – when in fact they can be full of sugar, preservatives and artificial flavours. There will always be better alternatives available, it just takes a little time to learn which ones to add to your supermarket trolley. As a simple rule of thumb, the shorter the list of ingredients, the better it is likely to be for you.

Cans & Condiments

Balsamic vinegar, Beans (black, kidney, butter), Chickpeas, Chopped tomatoes, Coconut cream or coconut milk, Coconut oil, Dijon mustard, English mustard, Honey, Nut oil, Olive oil, Pastes (garlic, ginger, chilli), Peanut butter, Rice wine or mirin, Sesame oil, Soy sauce or tamari, Stock pots/cubes, Tahini, Tomato purée, Vinegar (cider, white wine, red wine)

Frozen

Breads (wraps, flatbreads, pittas), Edamame (soya) beans, Peas, Raw peeled king prawns (dishes made with frozen prawns should not be re-frozen), Puff pastry, Sweetcorn kernels

Spices

Bay leaves (dried), Black pepper, Ground cardamom or cardamom pods, Chilli flakes, Chilli powder (mild), Chinese five spice, Dried oregano, Dried thyme, Fennel seeds, Ground cinnamon, Ground coriander, Ground cumin Ground turmeric, Paprika, Ras el hanout, Sea salt, Sweet smoked paprika

Dried

Brown sugar, Cornflour, Fruits (dates, cherries, raisins), Mixed seeds, Noodles (dried medium egg noodles, vermicelli rice noodles), Nuts (unsalted flaked almonds, cashew nuts, pistachio nuts, mixed nuts), Orzo, Panko crumbs or white breadcrumbs, Wholemeal and white pasta (penne, spaghetti, fusilli, pappardelle), Plain flour, Porridge oats, Rice (white or brown basmati)

Swaps & Switches

We all run out of our most-used condiments from time to time and many families have to adapt for intolerances or allergies. Don't panic! Here are some helpful substitution ideas.

INSTEAD OF	USE
Balsamic vinegar	Red wine vinegar
Coconut milk	Block of creamed coconut dissolved in hot water
Cream	Crème fraîche, full-fat natural or Greek yogurt, mascarpone, coconut or vegan alternative – use full-fat as it is higher in protein and will not split
Eggs	1 tablespoon cornflour mixed with 2 tablespoons water for binding Milk for pastry brushing/glazing 4 tablespoons unsweetened apple sauce mixed with ½ teaspoon baking powder or 1 tablespoon ground flaxseeds mixed with 3 tablespoons water for baking
Fish sauce	Lime juice
Fresh ginger, garlic, chilli	Pastes, purées or jars of ginger, garlic and chilli
Fresh spinach	Frozen spinach – defrost, add to boiling water or add straight to soups, pies and curries
Gochujang paste	1 tablespoon soy sauce (or tamari) and ½ teaspoon chilli oil instead of 1 tablespoon gochujang paste
Milk	Almond or oat milk
Peanut butter	Sunflower seed butter, soy butter, pea butter, tahini
Plain or Self-raising wheat flour	Chickpea (gram) flour, gluten-free plain or self-raising or rice flour for baking Cornflour for thickening
Red wine	Balsamic vinegar (1 glass red wine = 1 tablespoon balsamic vinegar)
Shaoxing/Rice wine	Mirin, Chinese cooking wine, dry or medium white wine
Sugar	Honey or brown sugar
Tamari	Soy sauce
Tamarind	Lime juice
Worcestershire sauce	Soy sauce, tamari, oyster sauce or good beef stock

Key: Recipe Icons

Look out for these helpful icons on recipe pages to tell you about the recipe.

Air Fryer
Recipes that can also be made in the air fryer, with instructions provided.

Slow Cooker
Recipes that can also be made in the slow cooker, with instructions provided.

Batch Cooking
Recipes that can be made in large batches (then refrigerated or frozen) and enjoyed over multiple occasions. *See* page 8 for batch-cooking tips.

Freezable
Recipes that can easily be frozen.

Make Ahead
Recipes that can be prepared ahead and left covered in the fridge until ready to cook. Also recipes that can be both prepped and cooked ahead and either served cold or reheated when ready to serve.

Vegan
Recipes that are vegan friendly, or have a vegan-friendly adaptation possible. These recipes are also suitable for vegetarians.

Vegetarian
Recipes that are vegetarian friendly, or have a vegetarian-friendly adaptation possible.

Gluten-free
Recipes which are gluten-free, or can be adapted to be gluten-free.

Dairy-free
Recipes which are dairy-free, or can be adapted to be dairy-free.

Sauces, Marinades & Rubs

Sauces, marinades and rubs are a great way to liven up meat, fish, vegetables and noodles. They are typically made from store-cupboard staples and the opportunities are endless.

Don't be fooled into thinking a marinade is something that has to be left steeping in the refrigerator for hours or days. Just adding meat, fish, veg or tofu to a marinade for 15 minutes will add depth of flavour and tenderize red meats and chicken. If you do want to prep ahead, proteins and vegetables can happily sit in most marinades in the refrigerator for much longer. On pages 22–3 you'll find a table to help you use marinades and rubs to elevate your chosen base.

My sauces, marinades and rubs are all really versatile and almost all will pair well with any meat, vegetable or fish. So be creative and try out different combinations to find your own favourite pairings, or try one of my trusted combinations outlined in the table below. As well as pairing with protein or veg, the sauces can also be used in different ways. For example, the Thai-style Dipping Sauce can also be used as a salad dressing, the Hoisin Sauce goes beautifully with noodles and the Hollandaise Sauce can be paired with eggs for a luxury breakfast. These simple sauces, marinades and rubs should give you endless options for easy and delicious meals.

BASE	FLAVOURS
Beef	BBQ • Cajun • Chipotle • Garam Masala • Garlic and Paprika • Ginger, Garlic and Sweet Chilli • Greek-style • Hoisin • Hollandaise • Lemon and Caper/Olive Butter • Onion Gravy • Peri Peri • Teriyaki • Thai-style Dipping Sauce
Chicken	BBQ • Buffalo • Cajun • Chipotle • Garam Masala • Garlic and Paprika • Ginger, Garlic and Sweet Chilli • Greek-style • Hoisin • Katsu • Lemon and Caper/Olive Butter • Onion Gravy • Peri Peri • Teriyaki • Thai-style Dipping Sauce
Halloumi	Cajun • Chipotle • Garlic and Paprika • Ginger, Garlic and Sweet Chilli • Peri Peri • Teriyaki
Lamb	Cajun • Chipotle • Garam Masala • Garlic and Paprika • Greek-style • Onion Gravy • Peri Peri
Pork	BBQ • Ginger, Garlic and Sweet Chilli • Onion Gravy
Fish	BBQ • Cajun • Chipotle • Garam Masala • Garlic and Paprika • Ginger, Garlic and Sweet Chilli • Hollandaise • Katsu • Lemon and Caper/Olive Butter • Peri Peri • Teriyaki • Thai-style Dipping Sauce
Prawns	Buffalo • Ginger, Garlic and Sweet Chilli • Hoisin • Katsu • Teriyaki • Thai-style Dipping Sauce
Tofu	BBQ • Buffalo • Cajun • Katsu • Teriyaki
Veg	BBQ • Chipotle • Garam Masala • Garlic and Paprika • Ginger, Garlic and Sweet Chilli • Greek-style • Hollandaise • Katsu • Lemon and Caper/Olive Butter • Onion Gravy • Peri Peri • Teriyaki

Serves: 4

Katsu Sauce

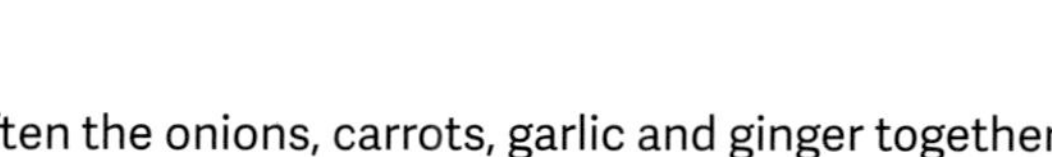

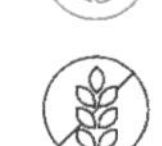

2 onions, chopped
2 carrots, chopped
3 garlic cloves, crushed
5cm (2 inch) piece of fresh root ginger, finely chopped or grated
2 tablespoons olive or groundnut oil
1 teaspoon ground turmeric
1 tablespoon curry powder (I used mild)
2 tablespoons honey
400ml (14fl oz) coconut milk
salt and pepper

Soften the onions, carrots, garlic and ginger together with the oil in a pan on a low heat for 10 minutes.

Add the turmeric and curry powder and stir, then add the honey and coconut milk.

Season with salt and pepper, then simmer for 10 minutes.

Blitz in the pan using a hand-held blender until smooth. Serve warm.

This can be frozen for up to 3 months. Defrost thoroughly and reheat in a saucepan on a low heat.

Serves: 6

Thai-style Dipping Sauce

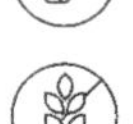

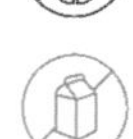

3 tablespoons hot water
3 tablespoons brown sugar
3 tablespoons fish sauce
3 tablespoons lime juice
2 chillies, deseeded and finely chopped
1 garlic clove, crushed
1 teaspoon chopped or grated fresh root ginger
3 tablespoons finely chopped fresh coriander

Stir together the hot water and brown sugar in a jug or bowl so the sugar dissolves.

Add all the remaining ingredients and stir well.

Pour into a clean jam jar, close the lid and store in the refrigerator for up to 7 days.

This can either be used as a dipping sauce or a salad dressing.

Serves: 4

Hollandaise Sauce

2 large egg yolks
2 teaspoons lemon juice
1 teaspoon white wine vinegar
150g (5½oz) butter

In a heatproof bowl, whisk together the egg yolks with the lemon juice and vinegar for a minute until light and frothy.

Melt the butter in a pan or microwave. Sit the bowl with the egg yolks over a pan of simmering water (don't let the bottom of the bowl touch the water).

Add the melted butter, little by little, to the egg yolk mix, whisking constantly until it thickens.

Take off the heat. The sauce can be served warm or chilled. Also tasty with eggs and gammon.

The sauce will keep in the fridge in an airtight container for up to 3 days. It can be gently reheated in a pan.

Serves: 4–6

Hoisin Sauce

4 tablespoons soy sauce or tamari
2 tablespoons smooth peanut butter
1 tablespoon honey
1 tablespoon brown sugar
2 tablespoons rice wine
1 garlic clove, crushed
¼ teaspoon chilli flakes
½ teaspoon Chinese five spice

Place all the ingredients in a bullet blender or a bowl with 3 tablespoons of water and either blend together or whisk by hand.

Add 1–2 tablespoons of extra water if needed to make it a drizzling consistency.

Transfer to a clean jar or bottle, close the lid and store in the refrigerator for up to 3 days.

This is great served with noodles.

Serves: 4–6

Onion Gravy

1 tablespoon olive oil
15g (½oz) butter
2 onions, sliced
2 tablespoons balsamic vinegar
2 teaspoons English mustard
2 tablespoons plain flour
600ml (20fl oz) stock (veg, chicken or beef, depending on what you wish to serve it with)
salt and pepper

Heat the olive oil and butter in pan and add the onions. Soften on a medium heat for 5 minutes before adding the balsamic vinegar. Cook for 2 minutes.

Stir in the mustard and flour, then gradually stir in the stock. Season, then simmer until thickened, stirring.

Great with mashed potatoes and pies. The gravy can be stored in an airtight container in the fridge for up to 3 days or frozen for up to 3 months.

Serves: 4

Lemon & Caper or Olive Butter

75g (2¾oz) butter
1 garlic clove, crushed
finely grated zest of ½ lemon and juice of 2 lemons
2 tablespoons (drained) capers or 100g (3½oz) pitted black or green olives, chopped
2 tablespoons chopped parsley (optional)
1 teaspoon salt
few grinds of pepper

Melt the butter in a pan on a low heat. Add the garlic and lemon zest. Stir, then add the lemon juice, capers or olives, parsley (if using) and the seasoning.

Cook on a low heat for 1 minute and serve warm.

The sauce can be kept in an airtight container in the refrigerator but will solidify. Reheat in a saucepan on a low heat, stirring continuously until the butter has melted.

Using Marinades & Rubs

Follow this simple table to create a flavour-packed meal using marinades and rubs with your chosen protein or veg.

To make the marinades, simply combine the ingredients and add to your chosen base, turn to coat, then leave for a minimum of 15 minutes and for a maximum of 1 day. If marinating for longer than 15 minutes, cover and leave in the refrigerator.

For the rubs, combine the ingredients and rub into your chosen base immediately before cooking.

Serve your cooked protein or veg with some veg – green salad, Tenderstem broccoli, green beans and asparagus all work well – and any other sides you fancy, such as cooked rice, pasta, couscous, beans, potatoes, bread, pitta or flatbread.

1. SELECT YOUR BASE

Chicken Breast
Flatten or butterfly to 2cm (¾ inch) thickness before adding marinade or rub.

Chicken Thighs
Leave whole or dice before adding marinade or rub.

Fish
Choose fillets of meaty fish such as cod, salmon, trout, sea bass, haddock or pollack, or flat fish like halibut or sole.

Halloumi
Slice widthways into 1.5cm (⅝ inch) pieces.

Lamb or Beef Steak
Flatten, if needed, to 2cm (¾ inch) thickness before adding marinade or rub.

Lamb Chop
Approximately 3cm (1¼ inch) thick.

Pork Tenderloin
Leave whole or slice into discs.

King Prawns
Defrost frozen prawns before patting dry with kitchen paper.

Tofu
Dry the tofu. If you have time you can press it by placing kitchen paper and something heavy on top. Cube or slice before mixing with the marinade or rub.

Vegetables
Use Mediterranean vegetables such as red onions, peppers, aubergines and courgettes, or root vegetables such as potatoes, carrots and parsnips. Try combining chickpeas, cooked lentils or beans with the vegetables. Chop the veg before adding rubs and marinades.

Use the flavour table on page 18 to help choose the best sauce, marinade or rub for your base!

Marinades and rubs are for 1kg (2lb 2oz) of base. Scale up or down as necessary. Marinades will keep for up to 3 days in the refrigerator in an airtight container and rubs for up to 3 months in an airtight jar in your store cupboard.

Fancy something saucy instead? Cook your base simply seasoned with salt and pepper, then serve with one of the sauces on pages 19–21.

2. SELECT YOUR MARINADE OR RUB

BBQ Marinade
1 heaped tablespoon smoked paprika, ½ teaspoon chilli flakes, 1 heaped tablespoon English mustard or 2 teaspoons mustard powder, 4 tablespoons tomato purée, 2 tablespoons balsamic vinegar, 3 tablespoons brown sugar

Buffalo Marinade
1 tablespoon ground cumin, 2 tablespoons smoked paprika, 1 tablespoon garlic granules (or use crushed fresh), 1 tablespoon brown sugar, 2 teaspoons salt, 3 tablespoons hot chilli sauce, 1 tablespoon olive oil

Ginger, Garlic and Sweet Chilli Marinade
2 teaspoons grated fresh root ginger, 2 garlic cloves, crushed, 4 tablespoons soy sauce, 3 tablespoons sweet chilli sauce, juice of 1 lemon, 2 teaspoons sesame oil

Greek-style Marinade
3 tablespoons olive oil, finely grated zest and juice of 1 lemon, 2 garlic cloves, crushed, 1 teaspoon dried oregano, 1 teaspoon dried rosemary or chopped fresh rosemary leaves, ½ teaspoon salt, few grinds of pepper

Teriyaki Marinade
2 tablespoons honey, 4 tablespoons soy sauce or tamari, 2 garlic cloves, crushed, 3cm (1¼ inch) piece of fresh root ginger, grated, 1 tablespoon rice wine, 1 tablespoon cornflour

Cajun Rub
1 teaspoon paprika, 1 teaspoon dried oregano, 1 teaspoon dried thyme, ½ teaspoon black pepper, ½ teaspoon cayenne pepper, ¼ teaspoon chilli flakes, ¼ teaspoon salt

Chipotle Rub
2 tablespoons brown sugar, 2 tablespoons ground dried chipotle pepper, 1 teaspoon paprika, 1 teaspoon mustard powder or English mustard, 1 teaspoon ground cumin, 1 teaspoon salt

Garam Masala Rub
¼ teaspoon garam masala, ¼ teaspoon salt, ½ teaspoon olive oil per fish fillet

Garlic and Paprika Rub
1 teaspoon garlic granules, ½ teaspoon salt, 1 teaspoon sweet, smoked or regular paprika

Peri Peri Rub
2 tablespoons paprika, 2 tablespoons garlic granules, 2 tablespoons ground coriander, 1 tablespoon salt, 1 tablespoon dried oregano, 2 teaspoons ground cardamom, 1 tablespoon smoked paprika, 1 teaspoon cayenne pepper

3. COOK

Chicken
Air Fryer: 190°C/375°F, 12 minutes for breasts, 15 minutes for thighs, turning both halfway.
Frying Pan: Medium heat with a little oil, 8 minutes for breasts, 20 minutes for thighs, turning both halfway.

Fish
Oven: 200°C Fan/220°C/425°F/Gas Mark 7, 10–12 minutes for meaty fish, 8–10 minutes for flat fish.
Air Fryer: 180°C/350°F, 8–10 minutes for meaty fish, 6–8 minutes for flat fish.

Halloumi
Air Fryer: Hasselback a block of halloumi by making seven deep incisions across the top (do not cut through), 200°C/400°F, 15 minutes.
Frying Pan: Slice the halloumi into 1cm (½ inch) thick pieces, medium heat with a little oil, 2 minutes on each side.

Lamb or Beef Steak
Air Fryer: 190°C/375°F, 6 minutes, turning halfway.
Frying Pan: Medium heat with a little oil, 3 minutes on each side. Rest, covered, for 5–10 minutes.

Lamb Chop
Oven: 180°C Fan/200°C/400°F/Gas Mark 6, 30 minutes, turning halfway.
Air Fryer: 190°C/375°F, 9 minutes, turning after 5 minutes.

Pork Tenderloin
Oven: 200°C Fan/220°C/425°F/Gas Mark 7, 35 minutes.
Air Fryer: 200°C/400°F, 22 minutes, turning halfway.
Frying Pan or Barbecue: Medium heat with a little oil, 25 minutes, turning every few minutes.

King Prawns (raw, peeled)
Air Fryer: 190°C/375°F, 4 minutes.
Frying Pan: Medium heat with a little oil, 4 minutes, turning halfway through.

Tofu
Air Fryer: 200°C/400°F, 12 minutes, shaking the drawer halfway through.
Frying Pan: Medium heat with a little oil, 8 minutes or until golden.

Vegetables
Oven: 190°C Fan/210°C/410°F/Gas Mark 6½, 30 minutes for Mediterranean vegetables, 40 minutes for root vegetables.
Air Fryer: 180°C/350°F, 12 minutes for Mediterranean vegetables, 20 minutes for root vegetables.

Whether you are working from home, need lunch on the run or have long school holidays ahead, the importance of lunchtime seems to be experiencing a resurgence and our expectations are rising above the humble sandwich. This is a development to be welcomed, but it can be a challenge to pluck something out of thin air on demand – let alone make it tasty and healthy. The key is to begin by looking in the refrigerator to see what it has to offer, then get creative. The recipes in this chapter should give you some starting ideas to seriously upgrade your snacks and lunches!

Light Bites & Lunchtime Lifesavers

Stuffed Mushrooms
Granola Energy Bars
Baked Eggs
Gyoza Noodle Bowls
Beef Quesadillas
Spiced Chickpeas & Halloumi on 5-minute Flatbreads
Kimchi Rice
Sweet Chilli Crispy Chicken or Halloumi Burgers
Tortilla Quiche – My Favourite Five
Peanut Noodles
Sweet & Sour Drumsticks
Mix & Match Tacos
Chicken & Sweetcorn Soup

Prep time: 10 minutes | **Cooking time:** 15–18 minutes | **Serves:** 2

Stuffed Mushrooms

Growing up I remember my mum making stuffed mushrooms as a starter when she had friends for dinner. I love them as a side dish too, particularly with steak. But stuffed mushrooms are a meal in themselves and offer a great lunch choice. There are so many filling options but this chorizo and melted cheese combination works so well with the earthiness of mushrooms. Serve with couscous, toast or a side salad.

6 portobello mushrooms or 4 large flat mushrooms
1 garlic clove, crushed, then mixed with 2 tablespoons olive oil, or use garlic oil
large handful of fresh spinach, finely chopped
50g (1¾oz) cooking chorizo sausage, finely chopped, or chorizo crumb
¼ red pepper, cored, deseeded and diced
125g (4½oz) ball of mozzarella cheese, drained
1 tablespoon olive oil
salt and pepper

TO SERVE
Couscous Salad (*see* page 173)
green salad

Preheat the oven to 180°C Fan/200°C/400°F/Gas Mark 6. Line a baking tray with nonstick baking paper.

Clean the mushrooms with a piece of kitchen paper, then place on the lined baking tray, stalk-side up.

Season the insides with salt and pepper, then spoon over the garlic oil. Add the spinach followed by the chorizo and red pepper.

Top with torn pieces of mozzarella and drizzle over the olive oil.

Bake for 15 minutes for portobello mushrooms or 18 minutes for large flat mushrooms, until the cheese is golden. Serve with Couscous Salad and green salad.

Air fryer method: Preheat the air fryer to 180°C/350°F. Place the mushrooms directly in the basket and cook for 10–12 minutes.

ADAPTATIONS

- Swap the chorizo for rindless bacon or ham, or omit to keep vegetarian.
- Swap the mozzarella for feta (crumbled), Cheddar (grated) or a soft cheese such as Brie (diced).

TIP

The uncooked stuffed mushrooms can be kept in the refrigerator, covered, for up to 24 hours.

Prep time: 10 minutes, plus chilling | **Cooking time:** 5 minutes | **Makes:** 9

Granola Energy Bars

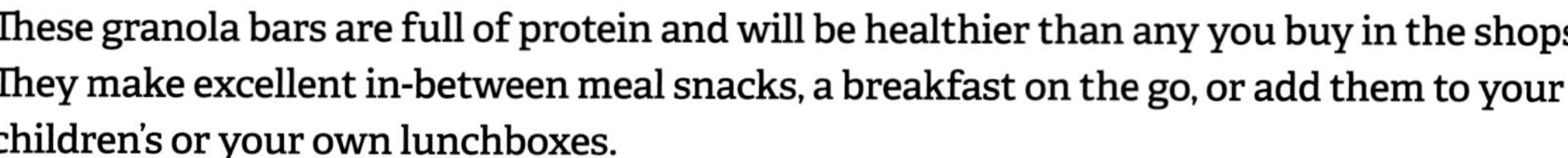

These granola bars are full of protein and will be healthier than any you buy in the shops. They make excellent in-between meal snacks, a breakfast on the go, or add them to your children's or your own lunchboxes.

225g (8oz) porridge oats
225g (8oz) pitted dates
5 tablespoons agave nectar, honey or maple syrup
6 tablespoons peanut butter
60g (2oz) coconut oil, melted
80g (2¾oz) blanched almonds, unsalted peanuts or hazelnuts, roughly chopped
80g (2¾oz) mixed seeds of your choice

Use a little of the coconut oil to grease a 20cm (8 inch) square cake tin, then line with nonstick baking paper.

Add the porridge oats to a large, dry frying pan. Toast on a medium heat for 5 minutes, stirring them periodically and keeping an eye on them so they don't burn. Tip into a large bowl.

Blitz the dates in a food processor. Alternatively, very finely chop them – they have to be very finely chopped to act as the sticking agent for the bars.

Combine all the ingredients together in the bowl with the toasted oats. Using a spatula, cut through the mixture so that the nectar/honey/syrup, peanut butter, coconut oil and dates coat the oats, nuts and seeds.

Add the granola mix to the lined cake tin and press down evenly. Refrigerate for 3 hours until firm.

Remove from the tin, cut into 9 equal squares and store in an airtight container in the refrigerator for up to 2 weeks. They can also be frozen for up to 3 months (defrost in the refrigerator before eating).

ADAPTATIONS

- To make granola, omit the peanut butter and add all the other ingredients except the dates to a bowl. Stir to combine, then tip on to a lined baking tray and spread out evenly. Roast in a preheated oven at 150°C Fan/170°C/340°F/Gas Mark 3½ for 20 minutes, stirring halfway through. Allow to cool. Add the chopped dates or dried fruits of your choice. Transfer to an airtight container and store at room temperature for up to 1 week.
- Use gluten-free oats for gluten-free energy bars.

Prep time: 5 minutes | **Cooking time:** 12 minutes | **Serves:** 1

Baked Eggs

An excellent source of protein, these baked eggs offer a great breakfast, brunch or lunch solution. The addition of halloumi, veg and bread makes these bowls a hearty meal.

2 teaspoons harissa paste
1 teaspoon olive oil
8 cherry tomatoes
large handful of fresh spinach, chopped, or 2 frozen spinach balls, defrosted
1 slice of sourdough bread, cut or torn into 4cm (1½ inch) pieces
60g (2¼oz) halloumi cheese, cubed
2 eggs

Preheat the oven to 170°C Fan/190°C/375°F/ Gas Mark 5.

Combine the harissa, oil, tomatoes, spinach, bread and halloumi in an ovenproof frying pan.

Make two wells in the mix and crack in the eggs. Bake for 12 minutes, or until the whites of the eggs are set and the yolk is still runny. Serve immediately.

Air fryer method: Combine the harissa, oil, tomatoes, spinach, bread and halloumi in a 15–18cm (6–7 inch) earthenware dish. Crack the eggs into two wells as above. Preheat the air fryer to 150°C/300°F and cook for 10 minutes.

TIP

Try swapping the halloumi for torn mozzarella, crumbled feta or grated Cheddar – simply sprinkle over the top before baking.

Prep time: 5 minutes (plus 5 minutes if making homemade stock) | Cooking time: 15 minutes (plus 10 minutes if making homemade stock) | Serves: 4

Gyoza Noodle Bowls

These noodle bowls are ready in 15 minutes – perfect for school holidays and weekends when the meal train seems never-ending. I also make this – sometimes minus the gyozas – when working from home for a quick lunch. I use shop-bought gyozas which I always keep in my freezer. As always, play around with the veg you add.

FOR THE HOMEMADE RAMEN STOCK (OPTIONAL)
1 litre (1¾ pints) chicken or vegetable stock
1 tablespoon chopped fresh root ginger (or use ginger paste)
2 garlic cloves, crushed
1 red chilli, deseeded and chopped
5 tablespoons soy sauce
3 tablespoons mirin (rice wine) or white wine
½ teaspoon Chinese five spice

FOR THE GYOZA NOODLE BOWLS
1 litre (1¾ pints) ramen stock (homemade or shop-bought)
1 tablespoon olive or groundnut oil
12–16 frozen gyozas of your choice
4 nests of dried egg noodles
200g (7oz) Tenderstem broccoli, chopped, and/or other green veg, such as mangetout and edamame beans
4 spring onions, trimmed and finely sliced
small handful of coriander, torn (optional)

TO SERVE
2 tablespoons soy sauce
chilli oil or sriracha

If making your own stock, add all the ingredients to a saucepan, bring to the boil, then reduce the heat and simmer for 10 minutes. Otherwise, pour the ready-made stock into a saucepan and bring to a simmer.

Heat a large, shallow pan until hot, then add the oil. Add the frozen gyozas straight to the pan, arranging them flat-side down. Colour on a medium heat for 5 minutes, then add 4 tablespoons of water to the pan and pop a lid on. Cook for a further 5 minutes.

Meanwhile, add the noodle nests to the simmering stock along with the broccoli. Simmer for 5 minutes.

Lift the noodles out of the pan into bowls, then ladle over the broccoli and stock.

Sprinkle with the spring onions and coriander, if using, then top with the gyozas. Finish with a little soy sauce and a drizzle of chilli oil or sriracha.

ADAPTATIONS

- Use vegetable stock and veggie gyozas for a vegetarian bowl.
- Use chicken stock and chicken/meat gyozas for meat eaters.
- Use vegetable stock and prawn gyozas for fish lovers.
- To ensure this is dairy-free, make sure you use dairy-free gyozas.

STAINLESS STEEL

Prep time: 15 minutes | **Cooking time:** 30 minutes | **Serves:** 4

Beef Quesadillas

These are one of my go-tos when I have a house full of teens. You can never make enough. It's not surprising as they incorporate three of my boys' favourite things – minced beef, wraps and cheese. With a batch of the filling ready cooked (you can use leftover Bolognese), they also make a great quick lunch. Or serve with chips/fries and salad for a heartier dinner.

1 tablespoon olive oil
400g (14oz) minced beef
1 heaped tablespoon chipotle paste
1 tablespoon chopped garlic
½ teaspoon salt
1 tablespoon dried mixed herbs
3 tablespoons tomato purée
200ml (7fl oz) beef stock
4 tortilla wraps
75g (2¾oz) Cheddar cheese, grated
couple of handfuls of fresh spinach, chopped
4 spring onions, trimmed and sliced
2 tablespoons sliced jalapeños (optional)

TO SERVE
guacamole
soured cream
chips or Crispy Fries (*see* page 182, optional)
salad (optional)

Heat the oil in a pan and add the beef, followed by the chipotle paste, garlic, salt and mixed herbs. Colour on a high heat for 5 minutes, breaking down the minced beef as it cooks.

Add the tomato purée and stock. Bring to the boil, then reduce the heat and simmer for 10 minutes until the stock has been absorbed and the beef has taken on a deep rich colour. Remove from the heat.

Spoon a quarter the beef mixture over one half of a tortilla wrap and top with a quarter of the Cheddar. Add some chopped spinach, some spring onion slices and jalapeños (if using). Fold the tortilla wrap over the filling so you have a semi circle. Repeat with the remaining wraps.

Heat a frying pan on a low heat. Add two quesadillas to the pan and cook for 2 minutes on each side. Carefully lift out onto a warmed plate. Repeat with the remaining quesadillas.

Cut each quesadilla in half and serve with guacamole and soured cream for lunch or with chips/fries and salad for dinner.

Air fryer method: Preheat the air fryer to 180°C/350°F. Place the quesadilla halves in the basket and cook for 6 minutes.

ADAPTATIONS

- Switch the minced beef for minced chicken, turkey or chopped chicken pieces.
- Use Quorn (and veg stock) for a vegetarian option.
- Double the quantities for bigger appetites.

Prep time: 10 minutes | **Cooking time:** 15 minutes | **Serves:** 2

Spiced Chickpeas & Halloumi on 5-minute Flatbreads

These two-ingredient flatbreads will become your flexible friend. They can be topped with all sorts of tasty ingredients from the refrigerator or served with hummus, but this chickpea, halloumi and tomato topping is my favourite way to serve them.

400g (14oz) can chickpeas, drained and rinsed
1 onion, finely chopped
2 garlic cloves, crushed
1 tablespoon extra virgin olive oil
1 heaped teaspoon ras el hanout
2 teaspoons balsamic vinegar
2 teaspoons honey
100g (3½oz) cherry tomatoes, halved
75g (2¾oz) fresh spinach, chopped (optional)
225g (8oz) block of halloumi cheese, cubed

FOR THE FLATBREADS
150g (5½oz) plain flour
150g (5½oz) full-fat Greek yogurt

Add the chickpeas, onion and garlic to a frying pan together with the olive oil. Cook on a medium heat for 5 minutes until the onion is softened.

Stir in the ras el hanout and balsamic vinegar and cook for 5 more minutes before adding the honey.

Add the tomatoes and stir. If using spinach, stir this through now. Push the chickpea mixture to one side of the pan, then add the cubed halloumi to the other side and colour for 5 minutes, turning every minute or so.

Meanwhile, for the flatbreads, combine the flour and yogurt in a bowl using a metal spoon. Bring the mixture together with your hands until you have a dough. Divide the dough in half and flatten each piece using your hands or a rolling pin so that each flatbread is 5mm (¼ inch) thick.

Heat a dry frying pan (you don't need any oil) on a medium heat. If using a large frying pan, you should be able to cook both flatbreads at the same time. Otherwise, cook one at a time. Add the flatbreads to the pan and cook them for 2 minutes on each side.

Transfer the flatbreads to plates, load the chickpea and halloumi mixture on top and serve.

TIP

The flatbreads can halved and reheated in the toaster, then topped, so you can make extra and store in an airtight container. They will keep for up to 3 days in the refrigerator and frozen for up to 3 months. They can be toasted directly from frozen or defrosted and reheated in a pan on a low heat for 1 minute on each side.

Prep time: 5 minutes | **Cooking time:** 10 minutes | **Serves:** 2

Kimchi Rice

The gut health benefits of kimchi are well documented. I'm not sure when I first discovered it, but although it's a relatively recent find for me, kimchi is one of those ingredients I now always have to hand. This kimchi rice is a fantastic refrigerator-raid lunch.

150g (5½oz) kimchi, including 3 tablespoons kimchi juice
2 tablespoons groundnut or other neutral cooking oil
1 tablespoon gochujang paste
400g (14oz) cooked rice of your choice – you can use a pouch or day-old rice (as long as it has been kept covered in the refrigerator)
1 tablespoon soy sauce or tamari
2 eggs
2 spring onions, trimmed and sliced lengthways

OPTIONAL ADDITIONS
chopped mushrooms, frozen peas, chopped leftover raw or cooked meat you have in the refrigerator (chicken, pork or beef), cut into small pieces

TO SERVE (OPTIONAL)
chilli oil
nori

Spoon the kimchi into a bowl. Press down with the back of a spoon and drain off the juice into another bowl. Pour off more kimchi juice from its container if you don't have 3 tablespoons.

Heat a wok or large frying pan and add 1 tablespoon of the oil. Add the gochujang paste and colour on a medium heat for 30 seconds. Add the kimchi. If using any of the optional additions, add these to the pan now too.

Cook for a few minutes, then add the cooked rice, the kimchi juice and soy sauce. Stir until the rice is heated through, about 3 minutes.

Meanwhile, heat the remaining oil in a frying pan, and crack the eggs into the pan. Cook on a medium heat for 2 minutes. If the bottom of the eggs is becoming crispy and the white on top is still runny, pop a lid on the pan and cook for a further 1 minute.

Serve the kimchi rice topped with the spring onions and a fried egg. I like a drizzle of chilli oil and a couple of nori sheets too.

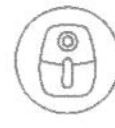
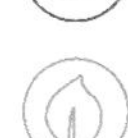

Prep time: 10 minutes | **Cooking time:** 6–22 minutes | **Serves:** 4

Sweet Chilli Crispy Chicken or Halloumi Burgers

A good burger never fails to hit the spot and these burgers are better than good! There's nothing complicated about them, but somehow they always feel decadent, particularly if you load both the chicken breast and a halloumi slice into one burger bun.

4 boneless, skinless chicken breasts and/or 225g (8oz) block of halloumi cheese, cut into 1cm (½ inch) slices
1 teaspoon salt
4 tablespoons sweet chilli sauce or chilli jam, plus extra to serve
100g (3½oz) panko crumbs, or use any breadcrumbs or crushed cornflakes
2–4 tablespoons olive oil (or you can use spray oil if cooking in the air fryer)

TO SERVE
4 tablespoons Greek yogurt (or use soured cream or mayo)
juice of 1 lime
1 garlic clove, crushed
4 burger buns, cut in half and lightly toasted
shredded lettuce

Mix together the Greek yogurt, lime juice and garlic in a bowl and set aside for serving.

Either butterfly the chicken breasts (slice widthways starting at the thicker part and ending at the thin point, being careful not to cut all the way through) or place them between 2 sheets of nonstick baking paper and bash out to an even 1cm (½ inch) thickness using a rolling pin. Cut each breast in half.

Spoon the sweet chilli sauce or jam into a bowl and add the chicken and/or halloumi. Stir gently to coat all over with the sauce/jam.

Tip the panko crumbs or breadcrumbs/cornflakes into a separate bowl. Dip each chicken piece and/or halloumi slice into the crumbs making sure it's well coated. Set aside on a tray lined with nonstick baking paper as you go. You can refrigerate the chicken or halloumi at this point, covering the tray in clingfilm.

If cooking on the hob, heat a large frying pan and add 2 tablespoons of olive oil. Cook the chicken on a medium heat for 3 minutes on one side, then turn it over. Cook for a further 8 minutes, turning the chicken every 2 minutes, until fully cooked through. You may need to do this in two batches.

For the halloumi, heat a frying pan, add the remaining oil and cook on a medium heat for 3 minutes on each side until golden.

Serve the chicken and/or halloumi in the burger buns with some shredded lettuce, the garlic-lime yogurt and some sweet chilli sauce drizzled over. Tuck in and enjoy!

Air fryer method: Preheat the air fryer to 180°C/350°F. Add the uncooked breaded chicken and/or halloumi to the basket and spray with the oil (2 sprays per breast, 1 per halloumi slice). Cook the chicken for 7 minutes on each side and the halloumi for 4 minutes on each side.

STAINLESS STEEL
MADE IN ENGLAND

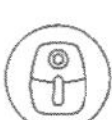

Prep time: 15 minutes | **Cooking time:** 20 minutes | **Serves:** 4

Tortilla Quiche – My Favourite Five

A modern take on the retro quiche, this is a great protein-packed meal. Once cooked, the quiche can be cooled and portioned for an on-the-run snack at any time of day. I've given you my favourite five combinations but raid the refrigerator and add what you love or need to use up.

olive oil or spray oil, for greasing/brushing
2 large tortilla wraps (25cm/10 inch diameter)
4 large eggs, whisked
salt and pepper

FOR SPINACH, BROCCOLI, FETA & MUSHROOM
3 broccoli florets, finely chopped
4 mushrooms, trimmed and finely chopped
50g (1¾oz) fresh spinach, chopped
75g (2¾oz) feta cheese, crumbled

FOR BACON, GOATS' CHEESE, PEA & ASPARAGUS
75g (2¾oz) frozen peas
100g (3½oz) asparagus spears, woody ends removed, chopped
50g (1¾oz) rindless bacon, ham or pancetta, chopped
75g (2¾oz) goats' cheese, crumbled or roughly chopped

FOR TOMATO, MOZZARELLA, OLIVE & BASIL
75g (2¾oz) sun-dried tomatoes, chopped
handful of pitted black or green olives, chopped
8 basil leaves, torn into pieces
150g (5½oz) mozzarella cheese, drained and torn into pieces

FOR PEPPER, CHORIZO, RED ONION & PARMESAN
¼ red pepper, cored, deseeded and chopped
½ red onion, sliced
75g (2¾oz) chorizo sausage, finely chopped or crumbled
50g (1¾oz) Parmesan cheese, grated

FOR CHEDDAR, ONION & HAM
3 spring onions, trimmed and sliced
50g (1¾oz) ham or rindless bacon, chopped
75g (2¾oz) Cheddar cheese, grated

Preheat the oven to 170°C Fan/190°C/375°F/Gas Mark 5. Oil a 20cm (8 inch) round cake tin or earthenware dish using olive oil or spray oil.

Lay the 2 tortilla wraps into the prepared tin/dish, pressing down around the bottom to form a case.

Add your chosen vegetables on top of the tortilla base. If using bacon, ham or pancetta, or olives and basil, or chorizo, add these too.

Add half of your chosen cheese to the whisked eggs together with a few grinds of black pepper. Season with salt, but go easy if using feta as it is already salty.

Pour the egg mixture over the base ingredients in the tortilla case. Finish with the remaining cheese.

Bake for 20 minutes, or until golden and the egg mixure is firm.

Remove from the oven, then carefully lift the baked quiche out of the tin/dish. Leave to sit for 5 minutes, then cut into wedges. Eat straight away or allow to cool, then store in an airtight container in the refrigerator for up to 2 days.

Air fryer method: Add the empty tin/dish to the basket and preheat the air fryer to 170°C/340°F. Brush or spray the tortilla wraps with oil and carefully lay them in the preheated tin/dish (as above). Repeat the steps above to fill the tortilla case then cover with foil. Cook for 10 minutes, then give the filling a gentle stir and cook for a further 7 minutes.

Prep time: 5 minutes | **Cooking time:** 5 minutes | **Serves:** 2

Peanut Noodles

There are no rules when it comes to making noodles. Anything goes. This sauce was adapted from my popular Hoisin Sauce recipe (*see* page 20) and is whisked together in less than a minute. You can keep this noodle bowl simple and stir the sauce through plain cooked noodles, or add some raw or stir-fried veg. For extra protein and to bulk the dish out for an evening meal, add some cooked meat, prawns or tofu.

2 nests of dried egg noodles

FOR THE PEANUT SAUCE
3 tablespoons crunchy peanut butter
3 tablespoons soy sauce
1 tablespoon rice wine
1 tablespoon honey
1 garlic clove, crushed
½ teaspoon Chinese five spice
¼ teaspoon chilli flakes (or 2 teaspoons sriracha)

FOR THE VEG (OPTIONAL)
1 carrot, cut into thin batons, peeled into strips using a potato peeler or grated
3 spring onions, trimmed, cut into thin strips
½ red pepper, cored, deseeded and cut into thin strips
¼ cucumber, cut into batons

Cook the noodles in a pan of boiling water for 4 minutes until tender, then drain.

Meanwhile, put all the ingredients for the peanut sauce in a bowl or jug, add 50ml (2fl oz) of water and whisk together.

Combine the hot noodles with half of the peanut sauce. (The remaining sauce can be frozen for up to 3 months or will happily sit in a covered bowl/jug in the refrigerator for a few days.) Stir through the raw veg (if using), divide between two bowls and serve.

ADAPTATIONS

- Stir-fry the carrot, spring onions and red pepper in a splash of olive or groundnut oil for a few minutes before adding the cooked noodles. Take off the heat and stir through the peanut sauce as above.
- Stir-fry strips of chicken, beef steak or pork, tofu cubes or raw peeled prawns (defrosted if frozen) in a splash of olive or groundnut oil, plus your choice of vegetables, until cooked. Stir through the cooked noodles. Take off the heat and stir through the peanut sauce as above.

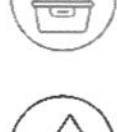

Prep time: 5 minutes | **Cooking time:** 45 minutes | **Serves:** 4

Sweet & Sour Drumsticks

You can never make enough of these, but in the unlikely event that they don't get hoovered up in one sitting, they're just as good cold. You can adapt the recipe for chicken wings too.

1kg (2lb 4oz) chicken drumsticks
1 tablespoon olive oil
4 tablespoons soy sauce or tamarai
2 tablespoons honey
2 tablespoons brown sugar
2 garlic cloves, crushed
1 teaspoon grated or finely chopped fresh root ginger, or use ginger paste
½ teaspoon Chinese five spice

TO SERVE (OPTIONAL)
sesame seeds
spring onions, trimmed and finely sliced
cooked rice
green salad

Preheat the oven to 180°C Fan/200°C/400°F/ Gas Mark 6. Line a roasting tray with nonstick baking paper.

Combine all the ingredients in a bowl, making sure the drumsticks are nicely coated, then transfer to the lined roasting tray, spreading the drumsticks out in a single layer. You can refrigerate the drumsticks, covered, for up to 24 hours at this point.

Roast for 45 minutes, turning the drumsticks over halfway through, until fully cooked.

Sprinkle with the sesame seeds and spring onions (if using) and serve. Or serve as part of a spread, or with rice and/or a green salad.

Air fryer method: Preheat the air fryer to 200°C/400°F and cook the coated drumsticks directly in the basket for 25 minutes, turning the chicken halfway through.

ADAPTATIONS

- You can swap the brown sugar for extra honey.
- Try using chicken wings in place of the drumsticks. Cooking times are the same.
- The recipe can be doubled if feeding a crowd or if you would like portions for the refrigerator which can be eaten cold.

Prep time: 10 minutes | **Cooking time:** 5–25 minutes | **Serves:** 4 (per protein option)

Mix & Match Tacos

Mix and match tacos are a great meal option if you have a fussy eater or have to cater for both meat eaters and vegetarians. Put everything on the table and let people build their own tacos.

12 mini soft flour tortilla wraps

FOR THE CHICKEN TACOS
4 boneless, skinless chicken breasts
2 garlic cloves, crushed
2 tablespoons olive oil
2 teaspoons chilli powder
1 teaspoon ground cumin
1 teaspoon smoked paprika
1 teaspoon dried oregano
½ teaspoon salt
½ teaspoon pepper

FOR THE BLACK BEAN TACOS
1 tablespoon olive oil
1 small onion, chopped
2 garlic cloves, crushed
1 red pepper, cored, deseeded and cubed
400g (14oz) can black beans, drained and rinsed
½ x 400g (14oz) can chopped tomatoes
1 teaspoon chipotle paste
1 tablespoon balsamic vinegar

FOR THE PRAWN TACOS
24 raw peeled king prawns, defrosted if frozen
1½ teaspoons chipotle paste
1 tablespoon olive oil

FOR THE HALLOUMI TACOS
2 x 225g (8oz) blocks of halloumi cheese, cut into cubes
2 teaspoons chipotle paste
1 tablespoon olive oil

TOPPINGS TO SERVE (OPTIONAL)
shredded lettuce
diced tomatoes
diced avocado flesh or guacamole
diced cored and deseeded red/yellow/green pepper
sweetcorn kernels
lime quarters
grated Cheddar cheese
soured cream, mayo or Greek yogurt

FOR THE CHICKEN TACOS
Either butterfly the chicken breasts or place them between 2 sheets of nonstick baking paper and bash out to an even 1cm (½ inch) thickness using a rolling pin. Combine the chicken with all the other ingredients until coated. Get a frying pan or griddle pan searing hot, then cook the chicken , in batches, on a high heat for 3 minutes on each side until fully cooked. Slice the chicken into strips.

FOR THE BLACK BEAN TACOS
Heat the olive oil in a pan, then soften the onion, garlic and red pepper on a medium heat for 5 minutes. Add the black beans, tomatoes, chipotle paste and balsamic vinegar, then simmer, uncovered, for 20 minutes until the sauce has thickend.

FOR THE PRAWN TACOS
Mix together the prawns with the chipotle paste and olive oil. Heat a frying pan or griddle pan until hot, then cook the prawns on a medium heat for 5 minutes, or until pink, turning regularly.

FOR THE HALLOUMI TACOS
Mix the halloumi with the chipotle paste and olive oil. Heat a frying pan or griddle pan, then cook the halloumi on a medium heat for 3–5 minutes, or until all sides are golden, turning regularly.

Meanwhile, prepare all your chosen toppings.

Warm the tortillas either in a hot oven or in a dry frying pan, according to the packet instructions. Or, to make rigid tortilla boats, preheat the oven to 180°C Fan/200°C/400°F/Gas Mark 6. Fold the tortillas loosely in half then nestle in the gaps of the underside of a 12-hole muffin tin to make an open-ended boat. Bake for 5 minutes.

Take everything to the table and let everyone load up the tortillas with their choice of filling(s) and toppings.

Prep time: 10–15 minutes |
Cooking time: 15 minutes or 2–6 hours hours (if making your own stock) | **Serves:** 4

Chicken & Sweetcorn Soup

This is my spin on a chicken and sweetcorn soup you may have tried from your local Chinese restaurant. Whenever I roast a chicken, I put the cooled, stripped carcass in the freezer. When I have a couple of carcasses, I add them to a pan straight from the freezer with an onion, carrot, herbs, peppercorns and plenty of water, then simmer on the hob or transfer to a slow cooker (*see* Tip below). But if that's all too much, just use good-quality shop-bought stock!

1 litre (1¾ pints) good-quality chicken stock (either homemade or shop-bought)
300g (10½oz) cooked chicken, chopped or shredded
100g (3½oz) sweetcorn kernels, either canned, frozen or cut off fresh cobs
3 tablespoons soy sauce or tamari
2 teaspoons sriracha (or use sweet chilli sauce)
1 garlic clove, crushed
2 teaspoons chopped fresh root ginger
2 eggs, whisked
5 spring onions, trimmed and chopped
sesame oil, for drizzling (optional)

To make the soup, add the stock, half the chicken and half the sweetcorn to a pan, together with the soy sauce, sriracha, garlic and ginger. Bring to a simmer. Remove from the heat and either blitz with a handheld blender, or transfer to a large blender, blitz, then return to the pan.

Add the remaining chicken and sweetcorn. Bring to a simmer and cook for 5 minutes, then add the whisked eggs. Stir and cook gently for 3 minutes so the eggs disperse in the stock, cook evenly and resemble threads. Serve in bowls and finish with the spring onions and sesame oil, if using.

TIP

To make your own stock, cover the cooked chicken carcasses with 2 litres (3½ pints) of water in a large pan. Add 1 chopped onion, 1 chopped carrot, 1 teaspoon black peppercorns, 2 tablespoon apple cider vinegar and a few sprigs of any fresh herbs you have. Bring to the boil, then reduce the heat and simmer, uncovered, for 2 hours. Or, better still, cook covered in a slow cooker on medium or in the oven at 130°C Fan/150°C/300°F/Gas Mark 2 for 6 hours.

Strain the stock before use and either use straight away or cool and transfer to an airtight container. The stock will keep in the refrigerator for up to 3 days and it can be frozen for up to 3 months (defrost overnight in the refrigerator before use).

When I'm meal-planning for the week, I have a subconscious rule for our dinners: it should be done in one pan, with minimal prep and ideally be ready in under an hour. If those boxes are ticked, then I know I won't still be stood at the hob at 9pm with an unruly crowd demanding their dinner.

There were staple fares when I was a child – Corned Beef Hash and Spaghetti Bolognese to name two – which were on weekly rotation. Fast-forward 30 years and my boys will happily eat Spaghetti Bolognese on repeat, and it acts like a culinary reset switch for them if they are having a bad day.

This Weekday Wonders chapter offers a selection of quick and easy dinners which will breathe new life into your typical meal rotation.

Weekday Wonders

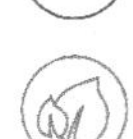

Prep time: 10 minutes | **Cooking time:** 25 minutes | **Serves:** 6

Chilli Two Ways

Here are two great alternatives to a classic beef chilli. Using minced chicken (which is lean and cooks quickly) and chipotle paste in place of numerous dried spices makes a quick and easy dinner, and the veggie/vegan version is ridiculously healthy, rich and hearty.

1 tablespoon olive oil
1 large onion, chopped
3 garlic cloves, crushed

FOR THE CHICKEN CHILLI
1kg (2lb 4oz) minced chicken
1 heaped tablespoon chipotle paste (2 tablespoons if you like more heat)
1 heaped tablespoon tomato purée
1 heaped tablespoon brown sugar
2 peppers (any colour, or mixed colours), cored, deseeded and chopped
2 x 400g (14oz) cans chopped tomatoes
400g (14oz) can kidney beans, drained and rinsed
200ml (7fl oz) chicken stock
salt and pepper

FOR THE CHICKPEA & BEAN CHILLI
3 peppers (any colour, or mixed colours), cored, deseeded and chopped
2 tablespoons balsamic vinegar
2 tablespoons chipotle paste
400g (14oz) can black beans or kidney beans, drained and rinsed
400g (14oz) can chickpeas, drained and rinsed
2 x 400g (14oz) cans chopped tomatoes
200ml (7fl oz) vegetable stock
1 teaspoon salt
few grinds of pepper

TO SERVE
chopped/sliced ripe avocado flesh
coriander leaves
lime wedges
cooked rice, warmed tortillas, tortilla chips or baked potatoes

Heat the olive oil in a pan and soften the onion on a medium heat for a few minutes, then add the garlic and cook for a minute.

FOR THE CHICKEN CHILLI
Add the minced chicken to the pan and colour for 10 minutes, breaking it up as it cooks. Season well then add the chipotle paste, tomato purée, brown sugar and peppers. Stir, then add the chopped tomatoes, kidney beans and stock. Bring to a simmer and cook, uncovered, for 15 minutes, or until the sauce looks rich.

FOR THE CHICKPEA & BEAN CHILLI
Add the peppers, then colour for 3 minutes before adding the balsamic vinegar, chipotle paste, black or kidney beans, chickpeas, chopped tomatoes and stock. Stir in the salt and a few grinds of pepper. Bring to a simmer and cook for 15 minutes, or until the sauce has reduced.

Serve the chilli with avocado, coriander leaves, lime wedges and either cooked rice, warmed tortillas, tortilla chips or baked potatoes.

TIPS
Serve leftovers in a wrap with some grated cheese.

This can be made ahead and freezes well. Both versions can be kept in an airtight container in the refrigerator for up to 3 days, and frozen for up to 3 months (defrost, then reheat before serving).

ADAPTATION
- For gluten-free, use a gluten-free stock cube or bouillon powder, but ideally use homemade stock (*see* Tip on page 49 to make my chicken stock).

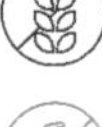

Prep time: 10 minutes | **Cooking time:** 50 minutes | **Serves:** 4

Lemon & Honey Chicken Traybake

This traybake takes minutes to throw together and after a stint in the oven you are rewarded with tender chicken meat, crispy skin, roasted potatoes and asparagus, plus lovely drizzling juices. Make this traybake when local asparagus is in season, or you can swap in courgettes or wilt in spinach right at the end.

3 lemons (juice from 2; remaining 1 sliced)
2 garlic cloves, crushed
2 tablespoons honey
2 tablespoons olive oil, plus extra for drizzling
2 teaspoons Dijon mustard
8 chicken thighs, skin-on, bone-in
750g (1lb 10oz) new potatoes, scrubbed and cut into 2cm (¾ inch) slices
400g (14oz) asparagus spears, woody ends removed
salt and pepper

ADAPTATIONS

- I love chicken thighs in this recipe as not only are they budget friendly and full of flavour, you also get caramelized crispy skin. But if you want to use boneless, skinless breasts/thighs, for the oven method, cook the potatoes in the oven first for 15 minutes, then add the chicken and lemon slices, season, drizzle over the lemon and honey mix and cook for another 25 minutes before adding the asparagus, drizzling with a little olive oil and squeezing over the remaining lemon half. Cook for 8 minutes.
- If using boneless, skinless breasts or thighs in the air fryer, preheat the air fryer to 190°C/375°F. Chicken breasts will need to be flattened first so they are evenly 2cm (¾ inch) thick. Toss the potatoes through half of the lemon and honey mix and tip into a liner or air fryer tray. Cook for 5 minutes. Give the potatoes a turn, add the chicken, lemon slices and the rest of the lemon and honey mix, season and cook for 8 minutes. Add the asparagus, drizzling with a little olive oil and squeezing over the remaining lemon half. Cook for 8 minutes.
- To make this gluten-free, make sure to use gluten-free mustard.

Preheat the oven to 190°C Fan/210°C/410°F/ Gas Mark 6½.

Squeeze the juice from 1½ lemons into a small bowl or jug. Add the garlic, honey, olive oil and Dijon mustard and mix together.

Arrange the chicken thighs (skin-side up) and potato slices in a roasting tin. Nestle in the lemon slices. Season well with salt and pepper.

Spoon over the lemon and honey mixture. Roast for 40 minutes.

Turn the chicken and potatoes over in the juices, then make space for the asparagus. You can just throw it on top!

Squeeze the remaining lemon half over the asparagus and drizzle over a little extra olive oil. Season and return to the oven for 8 minutes, until the chicken is fully cooked and the asparagus is al dente. Serve.

Air fryer method: Use a liner or tray and add the chicken (skin-side down) and the potatoes, then season. Pour over the lemon and honey mixture. Cook in a preheated air fryer at 190°C/375°F for 10 minutes, then turn the chicken over, give the potatoes a turn, add the lemon slices and cook for 10 minutes more. Add the asparagus and cook for 5 minutes more. If using a two-drawer model, you can cook the asparagus in the second basket and toss it through the chicken, potatoes and juices just before serving.

Prep time: 15 minutes | **Cooking time:** 25 minutes | **Serves:** 4

Teriyaki Meatballs

Teriyaki chicken skewers make a regular appearance on my weekday menu, so when I saw teriyaki lollipops on a restaurant menu, I couldn't wait to try them at home. They make a great canapé but are also really popular with my boys as an evening meal.

1 tablespoon groundnut oil, for frying (optional)

FOR THE MEATBALLS
750g (1lb 10oz) minced chicken
60g (2¼oz) panko crumbs or any breadcrumbs
1 tablespoon chopped fresh root ginger or ginger paste
1 tablespoon chopped garlic or garlic paste
2 tablespoons soy sauce
2 tablespoons finely chopped spring onions

FOR THE TERIYAKI SAUCE
2 tablespoons honey
4 tablespoons soy sauce
1 garlic clove, crushed, or 1 teaspoon garlic paste
1 teaspoon grated fresh root ginger or ginger paste
1 tablespoon rice wine
1 tablespoon cornflour, mixed with 3 tablespoons water

TO SERVE
cooked rice or noodles of your choice
lightly cooked green veg, such as pak choi or mangetout
3 spring onions, trimmed and sliced lengthways
1 tablespoon sesame seeds

The meatballs can be baked or pan-fried. If baking, preheat the oven to 200°C Fan/220°C/425°F/Gas Mark 7 and line a baking tray with nonstick baking paper.

Combine all the meatball ingredients in a bowl. Using your hands, divide and shape the mix into 16 golf ball-sized meatballs. Lay the meatballs on the lined baking tray.

Combine all the teriyaki sauce ingredients in another bowl, mixing well.

Either bake the meatballs in the oven for 20 minutes or pan-fry them in the groundnut oil on a medium heat for 10 minutes, then a low heat for a further 10 minutes. Ensure they are browned all over.

If oven-baking the meatballs, once cooked, transfer them to a hot pan.

Add the teriyaki sauce to the meatballs in the pan on a low heat. The sauce will caramelize very quickly. Turn the meatballs over in the sauce, adding splashes of water to loosen – you will need to add about 100ml (3½fl oz) of water to get a sauce that's sticky and coats the meatballs.

Serve with cooked rice or noodles and your choice of green veg. Sprinkle with the sliced spring onions and sesame seeds to finish.

TIPS

Making meatballs always takes a bit of effort, so for that reason I like to make them in a larger batch than needed. You can freeze the extra meatballs before cooking them. Lay them on a lined baking tray and open-freeze then, once firm, transfer to an airtight container or freezer bag and freeze for up to 3 months (defrost before cooking as above). You can also make the meatballs ahead and refrigerate them in an airtight container for up to 2 days before cooking. Make sure the meatballs aren't touching so that they don't stick together.

ADAPTATION

- You can make these vegetarian by substituting the minced chicken for Quorn mince and, for vegans, by also swapping the honey for agave nectar.

SCANPAN
SCANPAN

Prep time: 10 minutes | **Cooking time:** 25–55 minutes | **Serves:** 4

Pesto Chicken & Orzo Summer One Pan

Chicken and orzo combined with all things green make this a vibrant summer one-pan dinner. Adapt by adding any seasonal vegetables. I like to use chicken thighs in this recipe as you get that great crispy skin, but if you prefer to use breasts or even vegetarian or chicken sausages, you can cook this meal on the hob in 30 minutes.

8 chicken thighs, skin-on, bone-in (or use 4 boneless, skinless chicken breasts or 8 vegetarian or chicken sausages)
1 tablespoon olive oil
1 leek, trimmed, cleaned and sliced
300g (10½oz) asparagus spears, woody ends removed, stems chopped, tips reserved
700ml (1¼ pints) chicken (or veg) stock
4 heaped tablespoons pesto (*see* page 92 to make your own)
300g (10½oz) orzo
2 courgettes, sliced
100g (3½oz) frozen or fresh (shelled) peas, edamame or broad beans
salt and pepper

Season the chicken well. Heat the olive oil in a flameproof roasting tin on the hob, then add the chicken thighs, skin-side down, and brown on a medium heat for 10 minutes. Turn and cook for 5 more minutes. If using skinless chicken breasts or sausages, brown them for 2 minutes on each side.

Lift the meat (or sausages) out of the pan and set aside on a plate.

Add the leek, together with the chopped asparagus stems, to the pan. Cook for a couple of minutes on a medium heat, then stir in the stock and pesto.

If using chicken thighs, return them to the pan, skin-side up, then either simmer on the hob for 20 minutes or transfer to a preheated oven and cook at 170°C Fan/190°C/375°F/Gas Mark 5 for 20 minutes. Stir in the orzo and remaining veg (including the asparagus tips), then bring back to a simmer and either simmer on the hob for a further 20 minutes or return to the oven for another 20 minutes. Stir the orzo periodically to make sure it doesn't stick.

If using chicken breasts or sausages, add these, the orzo and the remaining vegetables to the pan after the stock and pesto. They'll take just 20 minutes to simmer on the hob or 20 minutes in the oven, stirring occasionally as above.

Prep time: 10 minutes | **Cooking time:** 10 minutes | **Serves:** 4

Saltimbocca

Traditionally in Italy, saltimbocca is made using veal, but here I've used an equally tasty and lean cut of meat: pork loin steaks. You could use chicken breasts too. So quick and easy to prepare, this dinner goes with mashed potatoes, baked potatoes or cooked rice and greens. Once the meat is resting, you can prep the delicious drizzling sauce in minutes.

4 pork loin steaks (or you can use 4 boneless, skinless chicken breasts or veal escalopes)
8 sage leaves
4–8 slices of prosciutto
1 tablespoon olive oil (or use spray oil, if air-frying)
175ml (6fl oz) white wine
175ml (6fl oz) chicken stock
50g (1¾oz) butter
salt and pepper

TO SERVE
Green Beans Almondine (*see* page 180) or Braised Cabbage and Peas (*see* page 178) or green salad
mashed or baked potatoes or cooked rice

ADAPTATION

- For gluten-free, use a gluten-free stock cube or bouillon powder, but ideally use homemade stock (*see* Tip on page 49 to make my homemade chicken stock).

If using chicken breasts, flatten each one to 1.5cm (⅝ inch) thick or butterfly them (slice widthways starting at the thicker part and ending at the thin point, being careful not to cut all the way through) Open out then cut each breast in half so you have 8 pieces of chicken.

Season the meat and lay 2 sage leaves on each pork loin steak (or veal escalope), or 1 on each chicken breast half. Wrap each piece of meat in the prosciutto slices.

Heat the olive oil in a large frying pan and add the meat. Cook the pork loin steaks (or veal escalopes) on a medium heat for 6 minutes, turning a few times so the prosciutto doesn't burn. Or cook the chicken breast halves for 8 minutes, turning every 2 minutes. Set the meat aside on a plate and keep warm.

Turn up the heat and add the wine to the pan. Let it reduce for a minute, then add the stock and bring to a simmer. Once the sauce is simmering, add the butter and then take the pan off the heat. Stir until the butter has melted and the sauce is glossy.

Return the meat to the pan to coat in the sauce. Serve with the veg or salad and potatoes or rice.

Air fryer method, for the meat: Preheat the air fryer to 200°C/400°F. Place the prosciutto-wrapped pieces in the basket, spray with oil and cook for 8 minutes. Once nearly cooked, make the sauce by adding the wine to a pan on the hob and following the instructions above, then serve the meat with the sauce spooned over.

Prep time: 10 minutes | Cooking time: 30 minutes | Serves: 4

One-pan Sausages & Beans

This is a lovely hearty yet healthy one-pan hob dinner that is cooked in 30 minutes. Perfect for busy midweek evenings.

1 tablespoon olive oil
8 chicken, pork or vegetarian sausages
2–3 rindless bacon rashers, chopped (optional)
15g (½oz) butter
2 leeks, trimmed, cleaned and sliced
2 garlic cloves, crushed
50ml (2fl oz) white wine (you can sub with juice of 1 lemon)
400g (14oz) can butter beans, rinsed and drained
400ml (14fl oz) chicken or veg stock
½ teaspoon chopped fresh or dried thyme
salt and pepper

TO SERVE (OPTIONAL)
green veg, such as peas or green beans
baked or mashed potatoes

Heat the oil in a pan and add the sausages. Colour on a medium heat for 5 minutes. Add the bacon (if using) to the same pan and colour for 2 minutes. Set the sausages and bacon (if using) aside on a plate.

Add the butter to the pan, followed by the leeks. Colour on a medium heat for 2 minutes, then add the garlic. After a minute, add the wine, let it bubble, then add the butter beans and the stock.

Season with salt and pepper and add the fresh or dried thyme. Return the sausages to the pan and top with the bacon (if using). Simmer for 20 minutes.

Serve with green veg and baked or mashed potatoes, if you like.

TIP
This one-pot is great for batch cooking and is ideal for freezing. Make it as directed, then cool and transfer to an airtight container. Freeze for up to 3 months (defrost before reheating to serve).

ADAPTATION
- Try adding 500g (1lb 2oz) whole baby new potatoes or sliced large potatoes. They can also be used in place of the butter beans. Boil for 10 minutes, then drain and add them to the pan with the stock and continue as above.

Prep time: 5 minutes | **Cooking time:** 18 minutes | **Serves:** 4

Asian-style Baked Sea Bass

This sea bass recipe always feels like a real treat, yet it is prepped and cooked on one baking tray and is ready in record time.

4 heads of pak choi, trimmed and halved
olive oil, for drizzling
4 sea bass fillets, skin-on, approx. 100g (3½ oz) each
about ¼ teaspoon Chinese five spice (a sprinkle on each piece of fish)
cooked rice or noodles of your choice, to serve

FOR THE SAUCE
5 tablespoons sweet chilli sauce
4 tablespoons soy sauce or tamari
2 teaspoons dark soft brown sugar
juice of 1 lime
1 garlic clove, crushed
1 teaspoon chopped fresh root ginger
1 red chilli, chopped (optional, for extra heat)
5 spring onions, trimmed and sliced

Preheat the oven to 200°C Fan/220°C/425°F/Gas Mark 7. Line a large baking tray with nonstick baking paper.

Lay the pak choi halves the lined baking tray and drizzle with a little olive oil. Bake for 10 minutes, then remove from the oven.

Meanwhile, mix all the sauce ingredients together in a bowl or jug.

Lay the fish fillets, skin-side down, next to the pak choi on the baking tray. Sprinkle the Chinese five spice over the sea bass. Go easy as it can be overpowering. Spoon the sauce over the fish and the pak choi.

Return the baking tray to the oven and bake for a further 8 minutes. The fish should be flaky and slightly sticky on top.

Serve with cooked rice or noodles, drizzling over the juices from the baking tray.

Air fryer method: Both the fish and pak choi will take 7 minutes in a preheated air fryer at 190°C/375°F. Depending on your air fryer capacity, you will most likely need to cook the pak choi and fish separately. Start with the pak choi – spooning over half the sauce before cooking – and keep it warm while you cook the seasoned fish with the remaining sauce spooned over.

Prep time: 10 minutes | **Cooking time:** 50 minutes | **Serves:** 4

Lentil Ragù

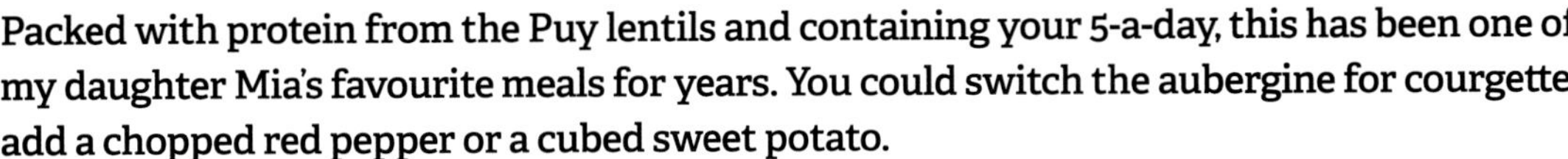

Packed with protein from the Puy lentils and containing your 5-a-day, this has been one of my daughter Mia's favourite meals for years. You could switch the aubergine for courgette, add a chopped red pepper or a cubed sweet potato.

1 tablespoon olive oil
1 large onion, chopped
3 garlic cloves, crushed
1 aubergine, finely chopped
2 carrots, finely chopped
100g (3½oz) mushrooms, trimmed and chopped
200g (7oz) dried Puy (green) lentils, rinsed
500ml (18fl oz) veg stock
1 tablespoon balsamic vinegar
1 tablespoon dried oregano
2 x 400g (14oz) cans cherry or chopped tomatoes
salt and pepper
grated Parmesan, Pecorino or hard vegan cheese, to serve

Heat the olive oil in a saucepan, then add the onion and soften on a medium heat for a couple of minutes. Add the garlic, aubergine, carrots and mushrooms. Soften all these for 5 minutes, then add the lentils, stock, balsamic vinegar, oregano and canned tomatoes. Season well with salt and pepper.

Bring to the boil, then reduce the heat and simmer, uncovered, for 40 minutes, adding a little water if needed, until the lentils are soft.

Serve with plenty of grated Parmesan, Pecorino or vegan cheese sprinkled over.

TIPS

This ragù is ideal for batch cooking and is perfect for freezing. Make it as directed, then cool and transfer to an airtight container. Freeze for up to 3 months (defrost before reheating to serve).

You can use ready-cooked lentils if you are short on time. Add them with half the quantity of stock and the remaining ingredients and simmer for 15 minutes.

ADAPTATIONS

- For gluten-free, use a gluten-free stock cube or bouillon powder, or use homemade veg stock.
- For dairy-free, omit the cheese for serving or use hard vegan cheese.

Prep time: 5 minutes | **Cooking time:** 10 minutes, plus resting | **Serves:** 4

Steak with Aji Verde

A steak dinner doesn't have to break the bank. Bavette (skirt steak) cooked quickly at a high temperature is a great budget cut. Serving it sliced with this Peruvian-style aji verde sauce alongside will deliver you a fantastic dinner in around 10 minutes.

4 beef bavette (skirt) steaks, each about 200g (7oz) and 2cm (¾ inch) thick (or use sirloin steaks), at room temperature
olive oil, for drizzling
salt and pepper

FOR THE AJI VERDE SAUCE
30g (1oz) fresh coriander
2 jalapeños, destemmed (seeds removed unless you like your sauce super-hot!)
1 tablespoon white wine vinegar
1 garlic clove
1 teaspoon salt
juice of 1 lime
½ teaspoon ground cumin
4 tablespoons mayonnaise

TO SERVE
salad
Crispy Fries (*see* page 182)

For the aji verde sauce, simply blitz all the sauce ingredients together in a blender and pour into a bowl.

Pat the steaks dry with kitchen paper and season generously with salt and pepper. Drizzle with a little olive oil.

Preheat a nonstick frying pan, griddle pan or barbecue until hot. Assuming the steaks are 2cm (¾inch) thick, brown the steaks on a high heat on both sides then sear the edges until cooked to your liking – approximately for 3 minutes on each side for medium rare, 4 minutes each side for medium and 5–6 minutes on each side for well done. Rest the steaks for at least 5 minutes before slicing.

Serve on individual plates or as a sharing platter with the aji verde sauce on the side. Serve with salad and Crispy Fries.

TIP
The aji verde sauce also goes well with pan-fried or griddled chicken, fish and prawns.

Prep time: 5 minutes | Cooking time: 30–70 minutes | Serves: 4

Sausage Ragù

Everyone loves a ragù, or a Bolognese as many of us now call it, but beef or pork versions are ideally cooked low and slow. This is a fantastic alternative cooked on the hob and it's ready in a little over 30 minutes. It's a recipe I know many of my Instagram followers have passed on to their kids when packing them off to university.

1 tablespoon olive oil
1 onion, chopped
3 garlic cloves, crushed
800g (1lb 12oz) good-quality pork sausages
1 teaspoon fennel seeds, crushed
1 teaspoon smoked paprika
½ teaspoon chilli flakes (optional)
100ml (3½fl oz) red wine (or 2 tablespoons balsamic vinegar)
400g (14oz) passata or canned chopped tomatoes

TO SERVE
baked potatoes or cooked pasta
grated Parmesan cheese
chopped chives

Heat a pan with the olive oil and add the onion and garlic. Cook on a medium heat for 5 minutes before squeezing the sausagemeat out of the skins into the pan. Discard the skins.

Break down the sausagemeat on a high heat and colour the mixture for 10 minutes. You want the sausagemeat to catch on the base of the pan and caramelize. Stir in the spices.

Add the red wine or balsamic vinegar to the sausage mix, let it bubble, then add the passata or chopped tomatoes. Simmer for at least 15 minutes. For a richer flavour, it can be simmered for up to 40 minutes if you have time.

Serve the sausage ragù with baked potatoes or pasta, sprinkled with grated Parmesan and finished with chopped chives.

ADAPTATIONS

- For dairy-free, simply omit the Parmesan, or use a hard vegan cheese instead.
- To batch cook, double or treble the quantities. It will keep in the refrigerator for up to 3 days. It can also be frozen for up to 3 months. Defrost and reheat in a pan.

Prep time: 20 minutes, plus (optional) chilling time | **Cooking time:** 15 minutes | **Serves:** 4

Thai-style Fishcakes

These will be the easiest fishcakes you ever make. For years I was put off sharing a fishcake recipe because typically they're a laborious task. These can be made up to 24 hours in advance, and for ease you can either use canned or fresh fish. Both are rich in protein, vitamin D and omega-3 fats.

4 tablespoons olive or groundnut oil, for frying, or use spray cooking oil for air-frying

FOR THE FISHCAKES
2 x 170g (6oz) cans salmon (skinless) or jumbo crabmeat, drained (or you can use 350g/12oz fresh skinless salmon or trout fillets, finely diced)
2 spring onions, trimmed and finely chopped
1 red chilli, finely chopped
finely grated zest and juice of 1 lime
2 fresh or dried lime leaves, shredded or finely chopped, plush extra to garnish
handful of fresh coriander, chopped
2 heaped tablespoons red curry paste
1 egg, beaten
2 tablespoons mayonnaise
150g (5½oz) panko crumbs or breadcrumbs

FOR THE COATING
100g (3½oz) plain flour
1 egg, beaten
100g (3½oz) panko crumbs or breadcrumbs

TO SERVE
Thai-style Dipping Sauce (*see* page 19) or sweet chilli sauce
Pan-fried Greens (*see* page 181) or Sautéed Broccoli (*see* page 179)
cooked noodles of your choice (optional)

Mix all the fishcake ingredients together in a large bowl until well combined. Divide and shape the mixture into 12 balls, then flatten them slightly. Place on a plate and pop in the refrigerator for 1 hour, if possible, to firm up.

To coat the fishcakes, roll each one in the flour, then dip in the beaten egg and then roll in the panko crumbs or breadcrumbs until coated all over (if making them in advance, place the fishcakes on a plate, cover and refrigerate for up to 24 hours, or freeze them – *see* Tip below).

To pan-fry, add the oil to a nonstick frying pan and heat until hot. Carefully add the fishcakes and cook on a medium heat for 10 minutes, turning them in the pan every few minutes, until evenly browned on all sides and cooked through.

Serve the fishcakes with the dipping or sweet chilli sauce, green veg and cooked noodles, and garnish with some extra lime leaves.

Air fryer method: Spray the fishcakes with oil, then cook in a preheated air fryer at 180°C/350°F for 15 minutes, turning them a couple of times to ensure they are evenly browned.

TIP
These fishcakes are great for batch cooking and freezing. Open-freeze the uncooked fishcakes on a tray then, once firm, decant into an airtight container or freezer bag. Freeze for up to 3 months and defrost in the refrigerator before cooking as above.

Prep time: 10 minutes | **Cooking time:** 30 minutes | **Serves:** 4

Gnocchi, Halloumi & Hidden Veg Sauce

People are often put off by gnocchi as it's associated with being tasteless and squishy. When it's simmered, I'm kind of in agreement! But here we have gnocchi with lovely crisp edges combined with halloumi cubes (and because they're baked they won't be squeaky!) cooked in a sweet tomato and vegetable-laden sauce. And it's all cooked in one pan in just 30 minutes!

splash of olive oil
1 onion, chopped
1 aubergine, finely chopped
1 courgette, finely chopped
3 garlic cloves, crushed
500g (1lb 2oz) ready-made chilled fresh gnocchi
225g (8oz) block of halloumi cheese, cubed
400g (14oz) can chopped tomatoes
400g (14oz) can cherry tomatoes (or a second can of chopped tomatoes)
½ teaspoon chilli flakes
100g (3½oz) fresh spinach, chopped
bunch of fresh basil, leaves picked and roughly chopped
salt and pepper
green salad, to serve (optional)

Preheat the oven to 180°C Fan/200°C/400°F/ Gas Mark 6.

Heat an ovenproof pan on the hob and add a splash of olive oil. Add the onion, aubergine, courgette and garlic and cook on a medium heat for 5 minutes.

Stir in the gnocchi and colour for a few minutes. Next add the halloumi and colour for a minute on all sides.

Pour in both cans of tomatoes, stir in the chilli flakes and season well with salt and pepper, then bring to a simmer. Transfer the pan to the oven and cook for 20 minutes.

Stir through the spinach and basil and serve with green salad if liked.

ADAPTATIONS

- You can play with the vegetable combo – any root veg will work, as will a red/orange pepper. My children claim to dislike aubergine and only one admits to liking courgette, yet no one notices them hidden in this sauce – just chop them very small or grate if you have a particularly discerning family member!
- Use gluten-free gnocchi to make this dish gluten-free.

Prep time: 5 minutes | **Cooking time:** 20 minutes | **Serves:** 4

One-pan Fish in Creamy Tomato Sauce

I always used to make this dish using salmon, but for variety I now often make it using a firm white fish or trout. Halibut is a real treat if you can source it. The fish is cooked in a Tuscan-inspired creamy tomato sauce and is delicious served with a green salad, bread or potatoes.

280g (10oz) sun-dried tomatoes in oil (weight with oil)
4 skinless fish fillets (such as cod, pollack, halibut, salmon or trout), each about 180g (6¼oz)
1½ teaspoons smoked paprika
1 small onion, chopped
3 garlic cloves, crushed
75ml (2½fl oz) white wine (optional – can sub with extra stock)
200ml (7fl oz) veg or fish stock
250ml (9fl oz) double cream (or sub with crème fraîche)
juice of ½ lemon
2 large handfuls of fresh spinach
1–2 tablespoons torn parsley leaves
salt and pepper

TO SERVE
rocket salad
Lemony Garlic Potatoes with Aioli (*see* page 184) or crusty bread

Drain the sun-dried tomatoes, reserving their oil as it's full of flavour, then roughly chop them.

Season the fish fillets well with salt and pepper, then sprinkle over ½ teaspoon of the smoked paprika.

Heat a nonstick frying pan until hot, then add 2 tablespoons of the reserved oil from the sun-dried tomatoes. Sear the fish fillets on a medium heat for 3 minutes on each side, then transfer to a plate and set aside.

Turn down the heat and add the onion to the pan. Soften on a low–medium heat for a few minutes, then add the garlic and remaining smoked paprika and soften for 2 minutes.

Stir in the wine (if using) and let it reduce for a minute or two, then add the sun-dried tomatoes. Pour in the stock, let it come to a simmer, then stir in the cream.

Add the spinach and stir through, then return the fish to the pan and simmer for 5 minutes, or until the fish flakes easily with the touch of a fork.

Finish with a squeeze of lemon and a sprinkling of parsley leaves. Serve with a rocket salad and Lemony Garlic Potatoes with Aioli (*see* page 184) or crusty bread.

TIP

You can use frozen fish. Just make sure the fish is defrosted thoroughly, then pat dry with kitchen paper, otherwise the fish will stick.

ADAPTATION

- For gluten-free, use a gluten-free stock cube or bouillon powder, or use homemade veg or fish stock, and serve with potatoes or gluten-free bread.

Is it just me who gets rather excited about the discovery of a new pasta shape? Pasta is frequently my fallback for a midweek meal and so I thought speedy recipes deserved their own chapter in this book. There are so many possibilities: from classics I have put my own stamp on, to recipes I have come up with completely by myself from years of cooking for pasta-loving children.

I am certainly not a pasta purist. The Italians will no doubt be disapproving of some of my creations and I happily switch between shop-bought dried and fresh pasta – life is far too hectic these days to be making my own.

Speedy Pasta

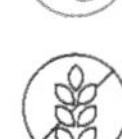

Prep time: 5 minutes | **Cooking time:** 20 minutes | **Serves:** 4

Arrabbiata

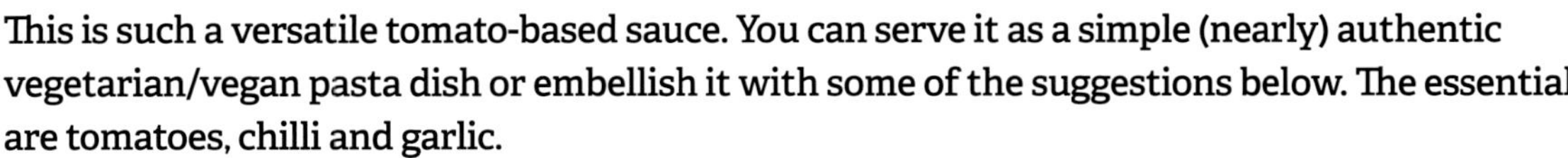

This is such a versatile tomato-based sauce. You can serve it as a simple (nearly) authentic vegetarian/vegan pasta dish or embellish it with some of the suggestions below. The essentials are tomatoes, chilli and garlic.

400g (14oz) penne, or pasta of your choice
garlic bread, to serve (optional)

FOR THE SAUCE
3 tablespoons olive oil
3 garlic cloves, crushed
½ teaspoon chilli flakes, or 1 large red chilli, chopped (including seeds)
1 tablespoon balsamic vinegar (or use 1 teaspoon brown sugar)
2 x 400g (14oz) cans chopped tomatoes
salt and pepper

Heat the olive oil in a pan, then add the garlic and chilli flakes/chilli. Cook on a medium heat for 1 minute, making sure the garlic doesn't burn.

Stir in the balsamic vinegar or sugar, then add the chopped tomatoes and season with salt and pepper. Simmer for 15 minutes.

Meanwhile, cook the pasta in a separate large pan of salted boiling water for 8–10 minutes, or according to the packet instructions, then drain.

Stir the pasta through the sauce to serve, or spoon the sauce on top of the pasta in bowls. Serve with garlic bread, if you like.

TIP
Batch cook the sauce by doubling all quantities. It will keep in an airtight container in the refrigerator for up to 3 days or frozen for up to 3 months. Defrost and reheat in a pan.

ADAPTATIONS
- Add some frozen peas to the tomato sauce for the last 6 minutes.
- Stir in some chopped spinach at the end to wilt in the heat.
- Add some shredded cooked chicken or cooked peeled prawns for the last 5 minutes to heat through.
- To make this gluten-free, use gluten-free pasta.

Prep time: 10 minutes | Cooking time: 10 minutes | Serves: 4

Creamy Smoked Salmon, Asparagus & Peas

Prep all the ingredients for this delicious pasta dish and the sauce is ready in the time it takes to cook your pasta. When local asparagus is out of season, substitute it with courgettes, chard or spinach.

400g (14oz) conchiglie, or pasta of your choice

FOR THE SAUCE
finely grated zest and juice of 1 lemon
300g (10½oz) crème fraîche
1 tablespoon olive oil
2 leeks, trimmed, cleaned and chopped
250g (9oz) asparagus spears, woody ends removed, stems chopped, tips reserved
100g (3½oz) frozen peas
150g (5½oz) smoked salmon, cut into strips
salt and pepper

Combine the lemon zest and juice and the crème fraîche in a bowl and set aside.

Cook the pasta in a large pan of salted boiling water for 8–10 minutes, or according to the packet instructions.

Meanwhile, heat a separate pan until hot, then add the olive oil, leeks and asparagus stems. Cook on a medium heat for 4 minutes before adding the asparagus tips and frozen peas. Season with salt and pepper and cook for a further 4 minutes.

Add the smoked salmon, stir, then take off the heat.

Stir through the lemony crème fraîche, adding a ladleful (75ml/2½fl oz) of pasta water to loosen.

Drain the pasta. Add the pasta to the pan, toss together with the sauce and serve.

ADAPTATION

- You can replace the smoked salmon with flaked cooked salmon or hot smoked salmon.
- To make this gluten-free, use gluten-free pasta.

Prep time: 10 minutes | **Cooking time:** 25 minutes | **Serves:** 4

Chicken & Chorizo

Despite having this on repeat for years, this is still one of my boys' favourite pasta dishes and in my top five go-tos for busy evenings, when I haven't followed my own advice and meal-planned!

400g (14oz) rigatoni, or pasta of your choice
grated Parmesan cheese, to serve

FOR THE SAUCE
2 tablespoons olive oil
200g (7oz) cooking chorizo sausage, thinly sliced
1 onion, chopped
2 garlic cloves, crushed
400g (14oz) boneless, skinless chicken breasts, cut into strips
400g (14oz) can chopped tomatoes
100g (3½oz) frozen peas

Heat the olive oil in a pan on a medium heat and add the chorizo. Let it take on some colour for about 2 minutes, then lift out and set aside on a plate, leaving behind the red oil the chorizo has released in the pan.

Add the onion and garlic to the pan and cook for 2 minutes.

Add the chicken strips and cook for 5 minutes, before adding the chopped tomatoes and returning the chorizo to the pan. Simmer for 15 minutes, adding the peas for the final 6 minutes.

While the sauce is simmering, cook the pasta in a separate large pan of salted boiling water for 8–10 minutes, or according to the packet instructions, then drain.

Stir the pasta through the sauce and serve with freshly grated Parmesan.

ADAPTATIONS

- For dairy-free, omit the Parmesan or use vegan hard cheese instead.
- Some torn mozzarella stirred through at the end is a delicious addition.
- To make this gluten-free, use gluten-free pasta.

Prep time: 5 minutes | **Cooking time:** 10 minutes | **Serves:** 4

Chilli & Lemon Crab

This is such a fresh pasta dish as the sauce requires no cooking. A few ingredients are simply combined while the pasta cooks, then you just stir the two together. A handful of green leaves adds another dimension but they can be left out and the pasta dish can instead be served with a side salad.

400g (14oz) linguine, or pasta of your choice
rocket or fresh spinach leaves, to serve (optional)

FOR THE SAUCE
300g (10½oz) fresh crabmeat (50:50 brown and white crabmeat is ideal)
2 large red chillies, deseeded and chopped
juice of 3 lemons
2 tablespoons chopped parsley or fresh coriander
5 tablespoons extra virgin olive oil
salt and pepper

Cook the pasta in a large pan of salted boiling water for 8–10 minutes, or according to the packet instructions.

Meanwhile, combine the crabmeat, chillies, lemon juice, chopped herbs and olive oil in a large bowl and season with salt and pepper.

Drain the pasta and toss it through the crab sauce.

Serve the pasta mixture as it is, or top with the rocket (if using) or wilt through the spinach (before serving).

ADAPTATION

▸ To make this gluten-free, use gluten-free pasta.

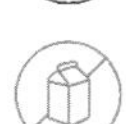

Prep time: 5 minutes | **Cooking time:** 50 minutes | **Serves:** 4

Roasted Tomatoes, Sweet Garlic & Mozzarella

This is a cracker of a summer pasta dish which makes the most of seasonal tomatoes and just a few other ingredients. Don't be put off by the whole garlic bulb – slow roasted, it becomes deliciously sweet and adds loads of flavour without being overpowering.

400g (14oz) farfalle, or pasta of your choice

FOR THE SAUCE
1 bulb of garlic
600g (1lb 5oz) cherry tomatoes
1 tablespoon balsamic vinegar
3 tablespoons olive oil
salt and pepper

TO SERVE
125g (4½oz) mini balls of mozzarella cheese, torn
handful of basil leaves

Preheat the oven to 150°C Fan/170°C/340°F/ Gas Mark 3½.

Sit the garlic bulb the right way up and slice just the top off so the cloves are exposed but the bulb is intact. Place, cut-side down, in a roasting tray. Add the cherry tomatoes, some seasoning, the balsamic vinegar and olive oil and slow-roast for 50 minutes, or until the tomatoes are soft and blistering and the garlic bulb is soft.

When the roasting mixture is nearly ready, cook the pasta in a large pan of salted boiling water for 8–10 minutes, or according to the packet instructions, then drain.

Squeeze the garlic flesh out of the skin into the roasted sauce and mix.

Toss the pasta through the roasted sauce, adding the torn mozzarella and finishing with the basil, then serve.

TIP

The roasted tomatoes and garlic also make a wonderful topping for toasted ciabatta.

ADAPTATIONS

- Torn mozzarella or burrata can be used in place of mini mozzarella balls.
- Omit the mozzarella for a vegan and dairy-free version.
- Cooked peeled prawns or cooked chopped chicken can be added to the dish. Add to the roasting tray for the last 5 minutes of cooking.
- To make this gluten-free, use gluten-free pasta.

Prep time: 10 minutes | **Cooking time:** 12 minutes | **Serves:** 4

Chicken Alfredo

I've embellished on this classic rich and indulgent creamy pasta dish by adding chicken and some peas. I feel that all family meals should really contain one veg. Feel free to leave out the chicken and swap in veggie hard cheese instead of Parmesan for a great vegetarian dinner (*see* Adaptation below).

400g (14oz) fettucine, or pasta of your choice
400g (14oz) boneless, skinless chicken breasts
pea shoots or chopped parsley, to serve

FOR THE SAUCE
100g (3½oz) frozen peas
1 tablespoon olive oil
30g (1oz) butter
2 garlic cloves, crushed
300ml (10fl oz) double cream
100g (3½oz) Parmesan cheese, grated
salt and pepper

Place the chicken breasts between two sheets of nonstick baking paper and flatten out to 2cm (¾ inch) equal thickness by bashing them with the end of the rolling pin. Season each chicken breast with salt and a little pepper.

Cook the pasta in a large pan of salted boiling water for 8–10 minutes, or according to the packet instructions. Add the peas for the last 4 minutes of cooking.

Meanwhile, heat the olive oil in a large frying pan and add the chicken breasts. Cook on a medium heat for 4 minutes on one side, then turn them over. Cook for 2 minutes, then add half the butter. Baste the butter over the chicken breasts and cook for 2 more minutes, or until cooked through, then set the chicken aside on a plate and keep warm.

Add the garlic and remaining butter to the frying pan. Once the butter has melted, stir in the cream and the Parmesan and season. Bring to a gentle simmer, then take off the heat. If the sauce is too thick, loosen with a little pasta water.

Drain the pasta and peas and add to the sauce. Use tongs to make sure the pasta is well coated.

Slice the chicken breasts. Divide the creamy pasta between bowls and top with the chicken slices and a sprinkle of pea shoots or parsley.

ADAPTATIONS

- If making the vegetarian version, omit the chicken and olive oil and substitute the Parmesan for vegetarian Italian-style hard cheese. Melt the butter, add the garlic, cook for 2 minutes on a low heat. Season with black pepper, then stir in the cream and grated veggie cheese and bring to a gentle simmer, before adding the cooked pasta and peas to the sauce.
- To make this gluten-free, use gluten-free pasta.

Prep time: 5 minutes | **Cooking time:** 10 minutes | **Serves:** 4

Spinach Pesto Pasta with Broccoli

Even veggie-lergic children won't notice the spinach hidden in this pesto. This recipe is a really simple way to load goodness into a pasta dish.

400g (14oz) casarecce, or pasta of your choice
200g (7oz) Tenderstem broccoli, stalks trimmed

FOR THE PESTO
60g (2¼oz) basil leaves, plus extra to serve
100g (3½oz) fresh spinach, chopped
200g (7oz) cashew nuts or pine nuts
100ml (3½fl oz) olive oil
juice of 1 lemon
2 garlic cloves
100g (3½oz) Pecorino, Parmesan or vegan hard cheese, grated, plus extra to serve

Cook the pasta in a large pan of salted boiling water for 8–10 minutes, or according to the packet instructions. Add the broccoli for the final 3 minutes, then drain.

Meanwhile, blitz all the pesto ingredients together in a blender until combined.

Stir the pesto through the pasta and broccoli, then serve with the extra grated cheese and basil.

TIP

This pasta is also great served cold, so make extra for lunchboxes. It will keep in the refrigerator for up to 2 days.

ADAPTATIONS

- Try adding some cooked chopped chicken, halved cherry tomatoes, chopped sun-dried tomatoes or pitted olives or mini mozzarella balls just before serving.
- To make this gluten-free, use gluten-free pasta.

Prep time: 10 minutes | Cooking time: 30 minutes | Serves: 4

Prawn Puttanesca

Thanks to the combination of olives, capers, anchovies and chilli, I'd describe an authentic puttanesca as robust and slightly fiery. My lot all claim to hate anchovies yet will devour my puttanesca sauce as long as I don't admit to including them! When finely chopped, anchovies almost dissolve and their job is to make the sauce richer and saltier, rather than fishy. I added prawns to this sauce but feel free to leave them out.

400g (14oz) spaghetti, or pasta of your choice

FOR THE SAUCE
1 tablespoon olive oil
1 red onion, chopped
4 garlic cloves, sliced
4 canned anchovy fillets, drained and finely chopped
50ml (2fl oz) white wine (optional)
400g (14oz) can chopped tomatoes
1–2 red chillies, chopped
½ teaspoon salt
10 grinds of pepper
2 tablespoons (drained) capers
60g (2¼oz) pitted olives, chopped
400g (14oz) raw king prawns, tail-on or peeled, defrosted if frozen (optional)

TO SERVE
basil leaves
rocket and Parmesan salad, to serve (optional)

Heat the olive oil in a pan and cook the onion on a medium heat for 5 minutes before adding the garlic and anchovies. Cook for 1 minute.

Add the wine (if using) and let it bubble for a minute, then add the tomatoes and chillies, salt and pepper. Bring to the boil, then reduce the heat and simmer for 20 minutes so the sauce thickens.

Meanwhile, cook the pasta in a separate large pan of salted boiling water for 8–10 minutes, or according to the packet instructions.

Add the capers and olives to the sauce. You may need to add a splash of the pasta water if the sauce looks too thick. Add the prawns (if using) and cook for a further 5 minutes, or until the prawns are completely pink.

Drain the pasta, add it to the sauce and toss together to mix. Finish with the basil and serve with a rocket and Parmesan salad, if you like.

ADAPTATIONS

- Swap the prawns for sliced cooked chicken.
- To make this vegetarian, omit the anchovies and prawns.
- To make this gluten-free, use gluten-free pasta.

Prep time: 10 minutes | **Cooking time:** 10 minutes | **Serves:** 4

Mushroom Pappardelle

You can use any pasta you have for this dish but I like using pappardelle, tagliatelle or fettuccine, as the ribbons hold the sauce beautifully. The earthiness of the mushrooms works so well with the creamy sauce.

400g (14oz) pappardelle, or pasta of your choice
1–2 tablespoons chopped parsley

FOR THE SAUCE
1 onion, finely chopped
oil, for frying
4 garlic cloves, crushed
500g (1lb 2oz) mushrooms – ideally 250g (9oz) chestnut (trimmed and sliced) plus 250g (9oz) wild or exotic (trimmed and roughly torn)
15g (½oz) butter
100ml (3½fl oz) white wine (or sub with extra veg stock)
100ml (3½fl oz) veg stock
5 tablespoons crème fraîche, double cream or dairy-free alternative
3 tablespoons grated Pecorino, Parmesan or vegetarian hard cheese
salt and pepper

Cook the pasta in a large pan of salted boiling water for 8–10 minutes, or according to the packet instructions, then drain.

Meanwhile, in a separate pan, cook the onion in a little oil on a medium heat for a few minutes. Add garlic, mushrooms, butter and plenty of seasoning and cook for 3 minutes.

Add the wine (if using) and let it bubble and reduce for a minute, then add the stock. Reduce that for a minute before stirring in the crème fraîche or cream and most of the grated cheese. Take off the heat.

Using tongs, add the cooked pasta to the mushroom sauce and toss to combine.

Finish with the chopped parsley and serve with the remaining grated cheese sprinkled over.

ADAPTATIONS

▸ To make this gluten-free, use gluten-free pasta and gluten-free veg stock.

Prep time: 5 minutes | **Cooking time:** 10 minutes | **Serves:** 4

Prawn & Asparagus Orzo

King prawns, asparagus and cherry tomatoes are partnered here for this fresh and decadent 15-minute dinner. Orzo offers risotto vibes without demanding the time and effort.

400g (14oz) orzo
handful of basil leaves, to serve

FOR THE SAUCE
250g (9oz) asparagus spears, woody ends removed, stems chopped, tips reserved (or use sliced courgettes)
250g (9oz) raw peeled king prawns, defrosted if frozen
finely grated zest and juice of 1 lemon
1 tablespoon olive oil
1 teaspoon chilli flakes
200g (7oz) cherry tomatoes, halved
2 garlic cloves, crushed
15g (½oz) butter
50ml (2fl oz) white wine (optional – use the juice of an extra lemon, if preferred)

Cook the orzo in a large pan of salted boiling water for 8–10 minutes, or according to the packet instructions, then drain.

Meanwhile, add the asparagus stems and tips to a bowl with the prawns, lemon zest, olive oil, chilli flakes, tomatoes and garlic and toss to mix.

Melt the butter in a separate frying pan. Add the prawn and asparagus mixture and cook on a medium heat for 5 minutes, then add the lemon juice and wine (if using). Stir for a couple of minutes until the prawns are pink and the alcohol has evaporated.

Add the drained orzo to the pan and stir to mix, then finish with the basil and serve.

ADAPTATION

- For dairy-free, simply swap the butter for an extra tablespoon of olive oil.
- To make this gluten-free, use gluten-free pasta.

Some of the most popular recipes on my Instagram page are my versions of takeaway favourites. We live in an age where you can order nearly any cuisine imaginable to your door (unless of course like me, you live in the middle of nowhere!). Even if you do have the luxury of those new takeaway services, they are expensive and will be far less nutritious and satisfying than anything you can make at home. I should point out that the recipes in this chapter are created in homage to the real thing, as opposed to trying to be authentic.

Fakeaways

Cheat's Chicken Tikka Masala
Vietnamese-style Pork
Biryani Three Ways
Beef & Vegetable Stir-fry
Matar Paneer
Chicken Hariyali Baingan
Chow Mein
Pulled Lamb Shoulder & Saag Aloo Traybake
Gyros
Raisukaree Curry Three Ways
Chinese-style Prawns with Cashew Nuts & Broccoli
Lamb Rogan Josh
Aloo Gobi
Thai-style Pork Curry

Prep time: 10 minutes | **Cooking time:** 30 minutes | **Serves:** 4

Cheat's Chicken Tikka Masala

I know tikka masala is a British creation, but there's good reason why this family-friendly curry has become so popular. Sadly, takeaway and supermarket versions tend to be full of nasties. This is my much healthier version of Chicken Tikka Masala, and with no skewering or marinating it's ready in just over 30 minutes.

FOR THE PASTE
1 onion
3 red chillies
10cm (4 inch) piece of fresh root ginger, peeled
3 garlic cloves
bunch of fresh coriander, stalks included
2 roasted red peppers from a jar, drained
1 tablespoon tomato purée
1 tablespoon smoked paprika
1 tablespoon ground turmeric
2 tablespoons ground cumin
2 tablespoons ground coriander
1 tablespoon garam masala
1 tablespoon honey
1 tablespoon groundnut oil
1 teaspoon salt

FOR THE CURRY
2 tablespoons groundnut or olive oil
2 onions, sliced
3 garlic cloves, crushed
1kg (2lb 4oz) boneless, skinless chicken breasts, diced
600g (1lb 5oz) passata or canned chopped tomatoes
200g (7oz) Greek yogurt (or coconut yogurt or double cream)
juice of ½ lemon

TO SERVE
cooked rice
parathas
fresh coriander leaves
flaked almonds

For the curry, heat the oil in a large saucepan and cook the onions on a medium heat for 5 minutes. You want them to take on a bit of colour. Add the garlic and cook for a minute.

Meanwhile, blitz together all the paste ingredients in a blender or bullet blender, adding a little water to loosen, if necessary.

Add the chicken and paste to the pan with the onions and stir. Cook on a high heat for a couple of minutes so that the chicken starts to take on some colour.

Add the passata or chopped tomatoes, bring to a simmer then cook, uncovered, for 20 minutes.

Stir in the yogurt and lemon juice and serve with rice and parathas, sprinkled with coriander leaves and flaked almonds.

TIP
This curry is ideal for batch cooking and making ahead and it freezes well. Cool the cooked curry, then transfer to an airtight container and freeze for up to 3 months (defrost before reheating to serve).

ADAPTATIONS
- For dairy-free, use coconut yogurt.

Prep time: 10 minutes | **Cooking time:** 1 hour 50 minutes | **Serves:** 4

Vietnamese-style Pork

This Vietnamese-inspired dish has a slightly sweet and sour tang (thanks to the brown sugar or honey combined with sriracha, soy sauce and fish sauce) but isn't sickly sweet like some sweet and sour dishes. With a mild chilli hit, it's family-friendly too. Plus it's all cooked in one tray (as long as you own one that transfers from hob to oven).

800g (1lb 12oz) pork belly strips
2 tablespoons soy sauce or tamari
1½ tablespoons sriracha (or chilli sauce)
1 tablespoon rice wine (mirin)
3 garlic cloves, crushed
1 tablespoon finely chopped fresh root ginger
2 star anise
100ml (3½fl oz) chicken stock

TO FINISH
2 tablespoons brown sugar or honey
1 tablespoon fish sauce
1 teaspoon sesame oil
100g (3½oz) sugar snap peas, thinly sliced
4 spring onions, sliced
1 tablespoon unsalted peanuts, chopped (optional)
1 red chilli, chopped and deseeded (optional, for extra heat)
juice of 1 lime

Preheat the oven to 140°C Fan/160°C/325°F/Gas Mark 3.

Chop the pork belly into 4cm (1½ inch) pieces, trimming off any excess fat, but don't go mad – belly is a fatty cut.

Combine the pork, soy sauce, sriracha, rice wine, garlic, ginger and star anise in an ovenproof pan. Place on the hob on a medium heat, and once the meat starts to take on colour (after about 10 minutes), pour over the stock.

Transfer the pan to the oven, then cook for 1½ hours.

Return the pan to the hob. Add the brown sugar or honey, the fish sauce and sesame oil and cook on a high heat until the liquid reduces and the pork starts to look sticky, about 5 minutes.

Add the sugar snap peas and cook for another 2 minutes, finishing with the spring onions, peanuts and the chilli if you want more heat.

Squeeze over the juice of the lime for extra tang, then serve.

Prep time: 10 minutes | **Cooking time:** 20 minutes, plus standing | **Serves:** 4

Biryani Three Ways

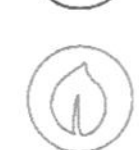

This is one-pot cooking at its best, whether you use chicken, salmon or make it vegetarian. This is a family-friendly version so double-up on the chilli if you want extra heat.

15g (½oz) butter
1 tablespoon groundnut oil
2 onions, chopped
4 garlic cloves, crushed
3 teaspoons grated or finely chopped fresh root ginger
1 red chilli, chopped
1 cinnamon stick
1 teaspoon ground turmeric
1 teaspoon ground cardamom
2 teaspoons ground coriander
2 teaspoons ground cumin
1 teaspoon salt
3 bay leaves
800g (1lb 12oz) boneless, skinless chicken breasts, cut into strips;
OR 800g (1lb 12oz) skinless salmon fillet, cut into large (4cm/1½ inch) chunks;
OR 400g (14oz) can chickpeas, drained and rinsed, 400g (14oz) mushrooms, trimmed and sliced, and 100g (3½oz) fresh spinach, chopped
2 tablespoons tomato purée
3 large tomatoes, chopped
300g (10½oz) white basmati rice
750ml (23½fl oz) chicken or vegetable stock

TO SERVE
2 tablespoons toasted flaked almonds
small bunch of fresh coriander, leaves and stalks roughly chopped
lemon wedges
yogurt

Add the butter, groundnut oil and onions to a large lidded pan and cook on a medium heat for 5 minutes before adding the garlic, ginger, red chilli, cinnamon stick, all the ground spices, the salt and bay leaves. Cook, stirring, for 1–2 minutes.

If using chicken, add this now. For the veggie version, add the chickpeas and mushrooms. Cook for a few minutes before adding the tomato purée, tomatoes, rice and stock. Stir, bring to a simmer, then cover and cook on a low heat for 10 minutes.

The rice should have absorbed most of the stock by now. Remove the pan from the heat, stir again, replace the lid and leave to sit for 10 minutes. Stir through the spinach at this stage for the veggie version.

For the salmon version, add the tomato purée, tomatoes, rice and stock, after the spices, salt and bay leaves, cover and simmer for 8 minutes. Add the salmon and stir it through. Cook for 2–3 minutes, then cover and leave to sit for 10 minutes.

Serve sprinkled with the toasted flaked almonds and fresh coriander, with lemon wedges and yogurt.

Slow cooker method: Cook the onions and garlic in the oil on high for 5 minutes first before adding all the remaining ingredients. Stir, cover and cook for 5–6 hours on low or 2–3 on high. The stock will have been absorbed by the rice and the chicken will be cooked through. Fluff up the rice using a fork before serving.

TIP
This can be batch cooked, made ahead and it freezes well. Cool the cooked biryani, then transfer to an airtight container and freeze for up to 3 months (defrost before reheating thoroughly to serve). All variations can be kept in the refrigerator for up to 24 hours. Reheat thoroughly in a pan, adding a little water if necessary.

ADAPTATION
- For gluten-free, use a gluten-free stock cube or bouillon powder, or use homemade veg or chicken stock (*see* Tip on page 49 to make my homemade chicken stock).

Prep time: 15 minutes | Cooking time: 8 minutes, plus marinating | Serves: 4

Beef & Vegetable Stir-fry

Get your Chinese takeaway fix at home with this super-easy beef stir-fry. Add any vegetables you like but I have provided some suggestions and directions for variety. You can make the sauce in a larger batch and keep it in a jar in the refrigerator for a couple of weeks. It goes well with chicken, tofu and prawns!

700g (1lb 9oz) beef steak (sirloin, rump, fillet or bavette)
1 tablespoon groundnut or vegetable oil
5 spring onions, trimmed and cut into 5cm (2 inch) pieces

FOR THE SAUCE
1½ tablespoons cornflour mixed with 4 tablespoons water
1 garlic clove, crushed
1 teaspoon grated fresh root ginger (or use ginger paste)
2 tablespoons brown sugar
2 tablespoons rice wine (mirin), Chinese cooking wine or sub with white wine
4 tablespoons soy sauce or tamari

VEGETABLE OPTIONS (USE A COMBINATION OF OR ALL OF THE BELOW)
1 red pepper, cored, deseeded and cut into strips
100g (3½oz) green beans, trimmed and cut in half
100g (3½oz) Tenderstem broccoli, stalks chopped, florets left whole
1 carrot, cut into thin batons or use a vegetable peeler to make strips
2 pak choi, trimmed and shredded

TO SERVE
cooked rice
1 tablespoon sesame seeds (optional)
sliced red chillies (optional)

TIP
If using the cheaper cuts of beef, such as rump or bavette, you can tenderize the steak by sprinkling 2 teaspoons of bicarbonate of soda over the steaks. Rub it in with the back of a spoon, leave for 30 minutes, rinse and dry with kitchen paper, then slice and cook as above.

Mix all the sauce ingredients together in a jug or a clean jam jar. Start with the cornflour and water, then add everything else and mix well. Set aside.

Trim the fat off the beef. Slice the beef into 1cm (½ inch) thick strips across the grain (typically cutting across the shortest width of the steak). This is important so that the steak remains tender when cooked quickly on a high heat. (*See* Tip below for tenderizing beef.)

Place the beef in a bowl with half of the sauce and stir to mix. Leave to marinate for 5 minutes, or you can do this ahead, then cover and refrigerate for up to 24 hours.

Heat a wok or heavy-based frying pan. When the pan is hot, add the oil. Add the beef and stir-fry on a high heat for 2 minutes. The beef should be coloured but not cooked through. Transfer to a plate and set aside.

Add a splash of water (about 50ml/2fl oz) to deglaze the pan, add the spring onions, then depending on which other vegetables you are using, add the red pepper, green beans and broccoli stems. Stir-fry for 1 minute.

Return the beef to the wok/pan and add the carrot and broccoli florets. Continue to stir-fry for a further 2 minutes. If using pak choi, add this now.

Add the remaining sauce, then stir-fry for another minute until everything is coated. You may need to add a little more water to loosen the sauce.

Serve with cooked rice and finish with sesame seeds and sliced red chillies for some heat.

Prep time: 10 minutes | **Cooking time:** 20 minutes | **Serves:** 4

Matar Paneer

This curry is my take on the Indian dish matar paneer. As well as being cheese-based, it's a really fresh curry and I've added some extra goodness with spinach.

450g (1lb) paneer cheese, cubed
1 teaspoon each ground cumin, ground coriander and ground turmeric
1 tablespoon groundnut oil
1 onion
5 fresh plum tomatoes or 200g (7oz) canned chopped tomatoes
1 tablespoon grated fresh root ginger (or use ginger paste)
4 garlic cloves
½ teaspoon salt
2 teaspoons garam masala
150g (5½oz) frozen peas
100g (3½oz) fresh spinach, chopped
juice of ½–1 lemon

TO SERVE
pappadoms or rice
mango chutney
cucumber, tomato and red onion chopped salad

In a bowl, toss the paneer in the ground cumin, coriander and turmeric and the groundnut oil until coated. Set aside.

Blitz the onion, tomatoes, ginger, garlic and salt together in a blender to make a paste.

Heat a pan until hot, then add the paneer cubes and colour on all sides on a medium heat, about 5 minutes. Remove from the pan to a plate, then add the paste to the pan. Let it simmer for 10 minutes, adding a splash of water to loosen it.

Add the garam masala and the frozen peas and return the paneer to the pan. Simmer for 5 minutes, then stir through the spinach.

Finish with the lemon juice and serve with pappadoms or rice, mango chutney and cucumber, tomato and red onion chopped salad.

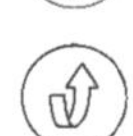
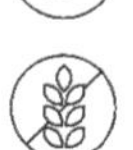

Prep time: 10 minutes | **Cooking time:** 50 minutes | **Serves:** 4

Chicken Hariyali Baingan

I have never seen this dish on any menu other than my local Indian restaurant, where it's become my favourite dish to order. It's a delicious, rich, medium-spiced and fragrant chicken and spinach curry which is served in a roasted aubergine. I understand *hariyali* means green curry and refers to the spinach, and *baingan* refers to the aubergine.

FOR THE CURRY
1 tablespoon olive oil
1 large onion, chopped
4 garlic cloves, crushed
4cm (1½ inch) piece of fresh root ginger, chopped
2–3 green chillies, chopped
2 bay leaves
½ cinnamon stick
¼ teaspoon whole cloves
2 teaspoons salt
1 teaspoon ground cardamom
2 teaspoons ground cumin
2 teaspoons ground coriander
1 tablespoon chilli powder
1kg (2lb 4oz) boneless, skinless chicken breasts or thighs, cut into 4–5cm (1½–2 inch) pieces
400g (14oz) can chopped tomatoes
1 tablespoon garam masala (plus a little extra to taste, if needed)
100g (3½oz) fresh spinach, chopped
salt and pepper

FOR THE AUBERGINES
2 aubergines
½ teaspoon garam masala
1 tablespoon olive oil

TIP

The chicken curry is perfect for batch cooking and making ahead and it freezes well. Cool the cooked curry, then transfer to an airtight container and freeze for up to 3 months (defrost before reheating to serve). Cook the aubergines fresh on the day you want to serve the reheated curry.

ADAPTATION

- You can serve this with cooked rice as a curry without the aubergines, if you prefer.

For the curry, heat 1 tablespoon of the olive oil in a pan until hot. Add the onion and cook on a medium heat, until it starts to colour, then add a splash of water and cook for 10 minutes more.

Add the garlic, ginger, chillies, bay leaves, cinnamon stick, cloves, the measured salt and all the ground spices (apart from the garam masala). Stir for a minute, then add the chicken.

Stir to coat the chicken in the spices. Colour on a medium heat for 5 minutes before adding the tomatoes, 100ml (3½fl oz) of water and the 1 tablespoon of garam masala. Bring to a simmer, then cook on a low heat for 30 minutes, or until the chicken is tender. Taste and add a little extra garam masala and salt, if needed.

Meanwhile, for the aubergines, preheat the oven to 190°C Fan/210°C/410°F/Gas Mark 6½.

Cut the aubergines in half lengthways and score the cut side in a criss-cross pattern. Season well with salt and pepper, sprinkle with the garam masala and drizzle with the olive oil. Place on a baking tray and roast for 40 minutes, or cook in a preheated air fryer at 190°C/375°F for 25 minutes.

Wilt the spinach through the curry, shred the chicken using two forks, then spoon the chicken curry over the aubergine halves and serve.

Slow cooker method, for the curry: Cook the onions in a little oil on a medium heat for 5 minutes. Add the garlic and cook for 1 minute, then add the ginger, chillies, all the spices, bay leaves, chicken, chopped tomatoes and seasoning. Cook on low for 6–8 hours or high for 3 hours. The chicken should be tender and the sauce should be rich and thickened. Stir through the wilted spinach.

Prep time: 10 minutes | **Cooking time:** 10 minutes | **Serves:** 4

Chow Mein

Quick, easy and a lot healthier than a takeaway, this chow mein is always such a hit whenever I cook it. You can switch the chicken for tofu or prawns, or load it with extra veg if you're looking for a meat-free option. I love a combination of chicken and prawns; if using both, half the quantities of each.

3 boneless, skinless chicken breasts, cut into 1cm (½ inch) wide strips;
OR 280g (10oz) firm tofu, cut into cubes;
OR 300g (10½oz) raw peeled prawns, defrosted if frozen
4 nests of dried medium egg noodles
1 teaspoon sesame oil
1 tablespoon groundnut or vegetable oil
1 onion, sliced
1 Chinese leaf cabbage, core removed, leaves shredded
1 carrot, cut into batons or use a vegetable peeler to make strips
100g (3½oz) bean sprouts

FOR THE SAUCE
3 garlic cloves, crushed
2 teaspoons finely chopped or grated fresh root ginger (or use ginger paste)
½ teaspoon Chinese five spice
1 teaspoon cornflour
3 tablespoons light soy sauce
2 tablespoons rice wine
1 tablespoon sweet chilli sauce

TO SERVE
4 spring onions, trimmed and sliced on the diagonal or shredded lengthways
prawn crackers

Mix all the sauce ingredients together in a bowl. Add the chicken, tofu or prawns and toss to coat in the sauce. Set aside.

Cook the noodles in a large pan of boiling water for 3–4 minutes, or according to the packet instructions. Drain and drizzle with the sesame oil so they don't stick together. Set aside.

Meanwhile, heat a wok or heavy-based frying pan until hot, then add the groundnut or vegetable oil. Add the chicken or tofu and the sauce. Stir-fry on a high heat for 5 minutes until the chicken or tofu is golden in colour. If using prawns, add them with the sauce and stir-fry for 2–3 minutes until they start turning pink.

Set aside the chicken, tofu or prawns on a plate, then add a splash of water to deglaze the wok/pan. Add the onions, cabbage and carrot. Stir-fry for 1 minute, then return the chicken, tofu or prawns to the wok/pan, along with the reserved noodles and the bean sprouts. Stir-fry for 30 seconds so that everything is heated through, then finish with the spring onions and serve with prawn crackers.

Prep time: 15 minutes | Cooking time: 4 hours 50 minutes–6 hours 50 minutes | Serves: 4

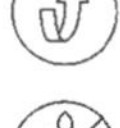

Pulled Lamb Shoulder & Saag Aloo Traybake

This is a true one-pan wonder, whether it's for a Friday night fakeaway, a Saturday night family treat or as an alternative to a Sunday roast. It uses a whole lamb shoulder slowly cooked to produce beautifully tender pulled meat, combined with potatoes which take on all the flavours from the lamb and gentle spices. Minimal effort required: the paste is whizzed up, spread over the lamb then everything is cooked in one roasting tray.

4 garlic cloves, crushed
5cm (2 inch) piece of fresh root ginger, grated
1–2 red chillies, deseeded and chopped
juice of 1 lemon
2 teaspoons ground turmeric
1 tablespoon ground cumin
1 tablespoon ground coriander
4 tablespoons Greek yogurt
1 whole lamb shoulder, bone-in, approx. 2.3kg (5lb 1oz)
2 onions, each cut into three discs
1kg (2lb 4oz) potatoes, cut into 5cm (2 inch) chunks
1 tablespoon garam masala
300g (10½oz) fresh spinach, chopped
salt and pepper

Preheat the oven to 140°C Fan/160°C/325°F/Gas Mark 3.

Combine the garlic, ginger, chillies, lemon juice and ground spices with the yogurt in a bowl.

Stab the lamb all over using a sharp knife and coat it in the spiced yogurt. Season with salt and pepper.

Lay the onion discs in a roasting tray and sit the lamb shoulder on top. Pour 200ml (7fl oz) of water around the edge of the lamb. Cover with foil, transfer to the oven and cook for 4–6 hours. The meat should be very tender and will pull apart with a fork.

Remove the foil, turn the temperature up to 160°C Fan/180°C/350°F/Gas Mark 4, then add the potatoes to the roasting tray. Sprinkle over the garam masala. Season with salt and pepper and toss the potatoes in the pan juices.

Return the roasting tray to the oven and cook for a further 50 minutes. By this time, the lamb should have taken on a lovely colour and be charred in places.

Stir the spinach into the roasting tray then serve the traybake, pulling the lamb from the bones to serve (discard the bones).

Slow cooker method: Place the onion discs in the slow cooker and add the potatoes. Sit the lamb shoulder on top, spread over the spiced yogurt and season, then cover and cook on medium for 6 hours, or on low for 8 hours or overnight. Stir in the spinach and serve as above.

TIPS

This traybake is great for batch cooking and making ahead and it freezes well. Pull the cooked meat off the bones (discard the bones) and cool the traybake, then transfer to an airtight container and freeze for up to 3 months (defrost before reheating to serve).

You can keep any leftover meat or potatoes in the refrigerator for up to 3 days. The meat is great served in wraps or pittas or used with the potatoes in salads

Prep time: 20–25 minutes | **Cooking time:** 35 minutes | **Serves:** 4

Gyros

A few years ago, we visited Greece on a family holiday and all became obsessed with gyros. You can make your own flatbreads and tzatziki easily, or use shop-bought for a shortcut.

1kg (2lb 4oz) boneless, skinless chicken thighs (approx. 8 thighs)
5 tablespoons Greek yogurt
3 garlic cloves, crushed
1 tablespoon smoked paprika
1 tablespoon ground cumin
1 tablespoon ground coriander
1 teaspoon cayenne pepper
1 teaspoon salt

FOR THE TZATZIKI
½ cucumber
1 garlic clove, crushed (or ½ teaspoon garlic paste)
4 tablespoons Greek yogurt
juice of ½ lemon
¼ teaspoon salt

FOR THE FLATBREADS
180g (6¼oz) plain flour, plus extra for dusting
1 teaspoon baking powder
180g (6¼oz) Greek yogurt
1 tablespoon olive oil, for oiling the pan

TO SERVE
green salad
chopped cherry tomato salad
sriracha
Crispy Fries (*see* page 182)

Preheat the oven to 180°C Fan/200°C/400°F/Gas Mark 6. Line a baking tray with nonstick baking paper.

Mix the chicken thighs with all the other ingredients in a bowl until coated. Fold and tightly thread each chicken thigh on metal skewers. Place on the lined baking tray and bake for 35 minutes. The chicken will be very tender so it can be pulled apart and will have taken on some colour.

Meanwhile, for the tzatziki, coarsely grate the cucumber and squeeze out the excess water. Combine with all other ingredients in a bowl, then set aside.

For the flatbreads, mix the flour, baking powder and yogurt together in a bowl using a fork first, then pull together and knead to form a dough. Divide into 4 and roll out each portion on a lightly floured surface so each flatbread is about 3–4mm (⅛ inch) thick. Heat a griddle pan or frying pan until smoking hot. Lightly oil it, then cook the flatbreads one at a time for 2 minutes on each side. There should be golden patches and some griddle lines if using a griddle pan.

Slice the chicken off the skewers. Load the chicken or halloumi slices on to the flatbreads with the tzatziki, some green salad, chopped cherry tomato salad and some sriracha. Pile the crispy fries on, or serve them alongside. Fold or wrap the gyros before serving. Tuck in and enjoy!

Air fryer method, for the chicken skewers: Lay in the basket and cook in a preheated air fryer at 180°C/350°F for 25 minutes, turning halfway through.

TIP
If you are in a hurry, skip the skewering and just pack the chicken thighs in tightly in a lined baking tray. Bake as above, turning once during the cooking time then shred/slice when cooked.

ADAPTATION
- For a veggie alternative, omit the chicken and yogurt and cut 2 x 225g (8oz) blocks of halloumi into 1cm (¼ inch slices). Combine with the garlic, spices and salt in a bowl. Heat 1 tablespoon of oil in a frying pan, add the halloumi and cook on a medium heat for 2 minutes on all sides or until lightly browned, or cook in a preheated air fryer at 180°C/350°F for 8 minutes, turning halfway through.

Prep time: 10 minutes | **Cooking time:** 12 minutes | **Serves:** 4

Raisukaree Curry Three Ways

Here's my simple and healthier version of raisukaree, the popular coconut-based curry. Chicken, tofu or prawns – all options are given here.

1 tablespoon groundnut or vegetable oil, plus an extra splash if using tofu
1 red onion, sliced
2 peppers (any colour), cored, deseeded and chopped
500g (1lb 2oz) boneless, skinless chicken breasts, cut into strips;
OR 280g (10oz) firm tofu, cubed;
OR 350g (12oz) raw peeled king prawns, defrosted if frozen
200ml (7fl oz) chicken or veg stock
400ml (14fl oz) can coconut milk, or use 100g (3½oz) coconut cream (in a block) dissolved in 400ml (14fl oz) hot water
100g (3½oz) sugar snap peas or mangetout
6 spring onions, trimmed and cut into 5cm (2 inch) pieces

FOR THE PASTE
3 garlic cloves
2 lemon grass stalks, trimmed and chopped
15g (½oz) fresh coriander
5cm (2 inch) piece of fresh root ginger, peeled
1 teaspoon ground cumin
1 teaspoon ground coriander
1 teaspoon hot smoked paprika
2 teaspoons honey or agave nectar
2 tablespoons fish sauce (sub with soy sauce for a vegan version)
1 tablespoon soy sauce or tamari
1 tablespoon groundnut or vegetable oil
juice of 1 lime

TO SERVE
cooked rice
sesame seeds
coriander leaves
1 red chilli, thinly sliced or chopped (optional – for extra heat)
lime wedges

Blitz all the paste ingredients together in a blender. Set aside.

Heat a wok or deep frying pan until hot, then add the oil and the red onion and cook for 1 minute on a high heat before adding the peppers. Cook for just 2 minutes then transfer the onion and pepper mixture to a plate and set aside.

If making the chicken version, add the chicken strips and the paste to the pan. Cook on a medium heat for 3 minutes.

If making the tofu version, colour the tofu first in an extra splash of oil on a medium heat for about 5 minutes, then add the paste and cook for a minute.

For the prawn version, add the paste and the prawns in the next step.

Add the stock to the pan together with the coconut milk or dissolved coconut cream. Bring to a simmer, then allow to reduce for a couple of minutes. If using prawns, add them now with the paste and cook for 1 minute. Add the sugar snap peas or mangetout, the spring onions and the onion/pepper mixture you set aside earlier. Simmer for 3 minutes, then serve with rice, sprinkled with sesame seeds, coriander leaves and chilli, if you like extra heat, and some lime wedges.

TIP
This curry (whichever version you make) is great for batch cooking and making ahead and it freezes well (but do not freeze if you have used frozen prawns). Cool the cooked curry, then transfer to an airtight container and freeze for up to 3 months (defrost before reheating to serve). The chicken and tofu versions will keep in the fridge for up to 3 days.

Prep time: 10 minutes | **Cooking time:** 10 minutes | **Serves:** 4

Chinese-style Prawns with Cashew Nuts & Broccoli

A brilliant Chinese fakeaway fix, I love this quick and easy stir-fry. The idea originates from a dish I ordered in my favourite fusion restaurant, but that version used batter. Most of us don't want to get the deep-fat fryer out, so here's an easier version that uses cornflour, egg and minimal oil for a delicate coating on the prawns.

24 large raw peeled king prawns, defrosted if frozen
1 tablespoon cornflour, seasoned with ¼ teaspoon pepper
1 egg, beaten
4 tablespoons soy sauce
2 tablespoons mirin (rice wine), Chinese cooking wine or sub with white wine
2 tablespoons groundnut oil
300g (10½oz) Tenderstem broccoli, stalks roughly chopped and florets left whole
4 tablespoons roasted cashew nuts
1 garlic clove, crushed
1 red chilli, deseeded and chopped
2 tablespoons honey
cooked noodles or rice of your choice, to serve

Toss the prawns in the seasoned cornflour to coat.

Whisk the egg together with 1 tablespoon each of the soy sauce and mirin/wine in a bowl. Add the prawns and toss to coat.

Heat the groundnut oil in a wok or frying pan and, when hot, remove the prawns from the egg mixture using a slotted spoon and add them to the pan. Stir-fry on a high heat for 5 minutes. Once the prawns have turned pink, lift them out on to a plate. Discard the leftover egg mixture.

Add the Tenderstem, cashew nuts, garlic and chilli to the pan. Stir-fry for a couple of minutes then return the prawns to the wok/pan, together with the remaining soy sauce and mirin/wine and the honey. Stir-fry for 1 minute then serve with noodles or rice.

ADAPTATIONS

- You can add asparagus, green beans or pak choi with or in place of the Tenderstem broccoli.
- For a chicken version, use 500g (1lb 2oz) chicken breasts cut into strips in place of the prawns and stir-fry on a high heat for 8 minutes.
- For gluten-free, use gluten-free cornflour and tamari instead of soy sauce.

Prep time: 10 minutes | **Cooking time:** 2½–4 hours | **Serves:** 6

Lamb Rogan Josh

A slow-cooked lamb rogan josh has long been one of my favourites to make for friends. Over the many years of making this, my recipe has evolved and it's now simplified into just a few steps. Yes, there are a quite a few ingredients involved but most of them are thrown into the paste. Cook it in the oven or in a slow cooker, or let it bubble away on a low heat on the hob.

FOR THE CURRY PASTE
5 garlic cloves
5cm (2 inch) piece of fresh root ginger, peeled
3 roasted red peppers from a jar, drained
1 tablespoon tomato purée
1 tablespoon smoked paprika
1 tablespoon garam masala
1 teaspoon ground turmeric
1 teaspoon salt
2 red chillies
1 tablespoon ground cumin
1 tablespoon ground coriander
1 teaspoon pepper

FOR THE CURRY
1 tablespoon olive or groundnut oil
1kg (2lb 4oz) lamb neck fillet or shoulder, diced
2 onions, chopped
2 tablespoons balsamic vinegar
75g (2¾oz) dried split red lentils
3 bay leaves
400g (14oz) can chopped tomatoes
800ml (28fl oz) chicken stock
salt and pepper
cooked rice or warmed flatbreads, to serve

Blitz all the paste ingredients together in a food processor or blender. Set aside.

Heat a large, ovenproof pan until hot, then add the oil. Season the lamb well then colour in batches in the pan on a high heat for about 5 minutes per batch, transferring each batch to a bowl, then set aside.

Add the onions to the pan and colour on a medium heat for 5 minutes. Add the balsamic vinegar, curry paste, lentils, bay leaves, chopped tomatoes and stock. Stir, then bring to a simmer.

Return the lamb to the pan, then cover and simmer for 2 hours until the lamb is tender, adding a splash more stock or water if it starts sticking.

Alternatively, transfer the simmering stew to a slow cooker, cover and cook on high for 4 hours, or cover the pan, transfer to a preheated oven at 130°Fan/150°C/300°F/Gas Mark 2 and cook for 4 hours.

Serve with cooked rice or warmed flatbreads.

TIP

This curry is great for batch cooking and making ahead and it freezes well. Cool the cooked curry, then transfer to an airtight container and freeze for up to 3 months (defrost before reheating to serve).

ADAPTATIONS

- You can use this recipe for a chicken, vegetarian or prawn rogan josh. For a chicken version, ideally use whole boneless, skinless chicken thighs and follow the recipe above. For a veggie option, colour the onions, then add the balsamic vinegar, curry paste, lentils, bay leaves, chopped tomatoes and veg stock. Add 800g (1lb 12oz) canned (drained and rinsed) chickpeas and 600g (1lb 5oz) combination of sweet potato, squash, aubergine or whatever takes your fancy, cover and simmer for 40 minutes. Or for a prawn version, use fish stock and let the sauce thicken and simmer for 30 minutes before adding 400g (14oz) raw peeled king prawns, defrosted if frozen, to cook in the sauce for a further 10 minutes.
- For gluten-free, use a gluten-free stock cube or bouillon powder, or ideally use homemade chicken (or veg) stock (*see* Tip on page 49 for my homemade chicken stock). Serve with cooked rice rather than flatbreads.

Prep time: 10 minutes | **Cooking time:** 15 minutes | **Serves:** 4

Aloo Gobi

Here's my take on the Indian-style vegetarian curry, aloo gobi. Featuring cauliflower and potatoes, it's hearty enough to have as a main course but you can serve it as a side to accompany another curry and rice, if you prefer.

1 cauliflower, cut into florets
2 tablespoons olive or groundnut oil
1 tablespoon black mustard seeds
2 onions, sliced
3 garlic cloves, crushed
5cm (2 inch) piece of fresh root ginger, peeled and chopped or grated
1 teaspoon ground turmeric
8 dried or fresh curry leaves
3 large potatoes, cut into 2.5cm (1 inch) chunks
1 red chilli, deseeded and chopped
200g (7oz) fresh tomatoes, chopped, or whole cherry tomatoes
150ml (5fl oz) vegetable stock
juice of 1 lemon
2 tablespoons chopped fresh coriander
salt and pepper

Preheat the oven to 180°Fan/200°C/400°F/Gas Mark 6.

Lay the cauliflower florets on a lined baking tray, season with salt and pepper, drizzle with 1 tablespoon of the oil and roast for 10 minutes, or until tender.

Meanwhile, heat the remaining oil in a large pan on a medium heat, then add the mustard seeds. When they start popping, add the onions, garlic, ginger, ground turmeric and curry leaves. Colour for a couple of minutes before adding the potatoes and red chilli. Cook for 10 minutes, stirring every few minutes.

Add the roasted cauliflower florets, the tomatoes and stock. Bring gently to the boil, then simmer for 5 minutes.

Finish with the lemon juice and fresh coriander, then serve.

ADAPTATION

▶ For gluten-free, use a gluten-free stock cube or bouillon powder, or use homemade veg stock.

Prep time: 10 minutes | **Cooking time:** 20 minutes | **Serves:** 4

Thai-style Pork Curry

Pork isn't commonly found in curries unless you turn to Southeast Asia. This Thai-style curry uses pork tenderloin, a super-lean and tender cut of meat. Even if you make your own green curry paste, this dinner is ready in about 30 minutes.

600g (1lb 5oz) pork tenderloin, sliced into 1cm (½ inch) discs
1 tablespoon groundnut or vegetable oil
3 heaped tablespoons Thai green curry paste (*see* below to make your own)
1 onion, sliced
3 tablespoons peanut butter
1 tablespoon brown sugar
1 tablespoon soy sauce or tamari
400ml (14fl oz) can coconut milk, or use 100g (3½oz) coconut cream (in a block), dissolved in 400ml (14fl oz) hot water
250g (9oz) green beans, trimmed

FOR THE THAI GREEN CURRY PASTE
4 green chillies, deseeded
1 shallot, roughly chopped
10cm (4 inch) piece of fresh root ginger, peeled and chopped
2 garlic cloves
30g (1oz) fresh coriander
2 lemon grass stalks, chopped
finely grated zest and juice of 1 lime
8 fresh or dried lime leaves, shredded
1 tablespoon ground coriander
1 teaspoon ground cumin
2 teaspoons fish sauce (or sub with the juice of an extra lime)
1 tablespoon groundnut oil

TO SERVE
cooked rice
small handful of fresh Thai basil leaves, to garnish
1 red chilli, thinly sliced

If making your own, blitz together all the ingredients for the Thai green curry paste in a blender (*see* Tip).

Heat the oil in a large pan until hot, then colour the onion on a medium heat for a few minutes before adding the measured curry paste.

Turn up the heat to high and add the pork. Colour for a few minutes, then add the peanut butter, brown sugar and soy sauce. Give everything a stir, then pour in the coconut milk or dissolved coconut cream and stir in the green beans.

Bring to a simmer, then cook on a low heat for 6 minutes. The sauce will have thickened. Serve with cooked rice and finish with the Thai basil and red chilli.

TIP
Store any leftover curry paste in an airtight container in the refrigerator for up to 1 week.

I'm comfortable admitting that at the weekends, when I have an influx of teenagers or friends visiting, although I want to provide a feast, I frequently embrace a shortcut. The heart may be keen, but the head is the ultimate pragmatist! I may have more time at the weekends to pre-plan a menu but I no longer find it necessary or practical to make that menu complicated. The one-pots, traybakes and platters still have their place, but I love curating a themed sharing feast too.

Weekends & Gatherings

Pot Pies Two Ways
Pork Fillet with Chimichurri
Moussaka
Smoky Beef Brisket with Coleslaw
Salmon & Tzatziki Platter
Tapas
Baked Meatballs Two Ways
Burrata, Nectarine & Giant Crouton Salad
Saffron & Prawn Risotto
Asian-style Pulled Pork
Spiced Chicken, Cauliflower & Lentil Traybake
Glazed Ham
Tartiflette
Lamb Shank Tagine
Prawn & Mango Noodle Salad
Pot-roast Chicken & Chorizo Rice
Harissa, Squash, Spinach & Feta Filo Tart
Pesto Cod in Parma Ham Traybake
Tandoori-style Chicken Salad
Slow-cooked Ox Cheeks in Red Wine

Prep time: 15 minutes | **Cooking time:** 35–55 minutes | **Serves:** 4–6

Pot Pies Two Ways

Everyone feels robbed when they get a pie that is tight on filling! When I came up with these recipes for chicken and vegetarian pot pies I had a picture of exactly how they should be – packed with veg in a lovely creamy sauce with a flaky pastry top. I like my pie with mashed potatoes and and seasonal cooked green veg, such as cabbage, broccoli or green beans.

1 tablespoon olive oil
500g (1lb 2oz) boneless, skinless chicken breasts or thighs, cut into 3cm (1¼ inch) cubes or strips (for the chicken pie);
OR 150g (5½oz) dried Puy lentils, rinsed, or 400g (14oz) pre-cooked Puy lentils (for the vegetarian pie)
15g (½oz) butter
1 leek, trimmed, cleaned and sliced
2 carrots, chopped into 1cm (½ inch) pieces
100g (3½oz) mushrooms, trimmed and chopped
2 teaspoons English mustard
2 tablespoons plain flour
100ml (3½fl oz) white wine (optional – can sub for more stock)
200ml (7fl oz) milk
200–300ml (7–10fl oz) chicken or vegetable stock, plus extra as needed
100g (3½oz) frozen peas
100g (3½oz) frozen sweetcorn kernels
2 tablespoons chopped tarragon
320g (11¼oz) ready-made puff pastry (sheet or block)
1 whole egg and 1 egg yolk, beaten
salt and pepper

TIP

The filling can be made ahead and refrigerated for up to 3 days, and frozen for up to 3 months if you want to batch cook it. Defrost before making the pies. Or the pies can be fully assembled and refrigerated for up to 24 hours.

ADAPTATION

- For a vegan version, make the vegetarian pie as above but substitute the butter with extra olive oil, replace the milk with plant-based milk, the wine with extra vegetable stock, top the filling with mashed potatoes instead of pastry (or use a vegan puff pastry) and omit the egg wash.

For the chicken pie, heat the olive oil in a pan and add the chicken. Season well with salt and pepper, then cook on a medium heat for 5 minutes, or until lightly coloured all over. Transfer the chicken to a plate and set aside. The chicken doesn't have to be cooked through at this stage.

Add the butter to the pan and let it melt, then add the leek, carrots and mushrooms. Cook on a medium heat for a couple of minutes before returning the chicken to the pan. Stir in the mustard and flour so the chicken is coated in the flour. Stir in the wine (if using) and let it reduce a little. Stir in the milk and stock. Bring to a simmer, then add the frozen peas and sweetcorn. Cook for 5 minutes. Take off the heat and stir in the tarragon and allow the mixture to cool. Preheat the oven to 180°C Fan/200°C/400°F/Gas Mark 6.

Spoon the chicken mixture into a 25cm (10 inch) round or 30 x 20cm (8 x 12 inch) pie dish and top with the pastry sheet, trimming it to fit (or roll out the pastry block to fit the pie dish), then flute the edges. Score the pastry lid or garnish it with offcuts of pastry cut into shapes of your choice (brush with beaten egg to fix them on to the pastry lid). Make an incision in the middle of the pie to let out steam. Brush the pastry with beaten egg and bake for 25–30 minutes, or until the pastry is risen, golden brown and crispy.

For the vegetarian pie, heat the olive oil and butter in the pan, add the leek, carrots and mushrooms, season well and cook as above. Stir in the mustard and flour followed by the wine (if using). Let it reduce a little, then add the milk, lentils, veg stock (if using dried lentils, use 600ml (20fl oz) of stock) and the frozen peas and sweetcorn. If using dried lentils, simmer for 20 minutes, otherwise simmer for 5 minutes, then stir in the tarragon. Allow to cool before topping with the pastry and baking in the same way as the chicken pie above.

Prep time: 10 minutes, plus marinating | **Cooking time:** 22–35 minutes, plus resting | **Serves:** 6

Pork Fillet with Chimichurri

Never the most attractive meat joint but always such a treat, pork fillet, or tenderloin, is very lean and takes minimal cooking. It's a great cut to cook in the oven or air fryer or on the barbecue. Here I've used a very simple marinade, then drizzled the pork with deliciously fresh chimichurri sauce once it's cooked. This is lovely with Lemony Garlic Potatoes (*see* page 184).

2 x pork fillets or tenderloins, weighing approx. 600g (1lb 5oz) each
2 tablespoons balsamic vinegar
juice of ½ orange or 1 clementine
salt and pepper

FOR THE CHIMICHURRI
40g (1½oz) mixed fresh coriander, oregano and parsley, leaves picked
1 red chilli, finely chopped (or use 2 for extra heat)
2 garlic cloves, finely chopped
3 tablespoons red wine vinegar
6 tablespoons extra virgin olive oil
½ teaspoon salt

Add the pork fillets/tenderloins to an ovenproof dish and add the balsamic vinegar and orange/clementine juice. Turn the fillets/tenderloins over in the marinade and season well all over. Leave to marinate for as long as possible. This can be done at room temperature for up to 30 minutes, otherwise cover and marinate in the refrigerator. Turn the meat over every now and then while it's marinating.

Preheat the oven to 200°C Fan/220°C/425°F/Gas Mark 7.

Cook the pork fillets/tenderloins in their marinade in the oven for 35 minutes, turning once or twice during the cooking time. Alternatively, cook them in a preheated air fryer at 200°C/400°F for 22 minutes. Or you can cook them on a preheated medium barbecue for 25 minutes, turning every 5 minutes and brushing with the marinade. Leave to rest for 10 minutes under tin foil. There should be juices running from the pork as it rests.

Meanwhile, make the chimichurri. Finely chop the herbs by hand then mix all the chimichurri ingredients together in a clean jam jar or a small bowl. Add more olive oil if needed to make it a thick drizzling consistency.

Slice the pork tenderloin and drizzle with the chimichurri to serve.

TIPS

Traditionally, chimichurri is fiery. My version isn't super-hot – it is a family-friendly heat. You can add an extra chilli if you want more heat. You can use whatever combo of fresh herbs you have in the garden or refrigerator drawer.

It's worth making the chimichurri in a larger batch than you need for this recipe. It will liven up cooked plain steaks, chicken, fish, potatoes (either roasted or boiled) and almost any vegetable. Store chimichurri in an airtight container or lidded jar in the refrigerator for up to 4 days.

Prep time: 25 minutes | **Cooking time:** 1 hour 45 minutes–7 hours | **Serves:** 6

Moussaka

There aren't many shortcuts you can take when making this Greek classic, but rest assured that I've made it as simple as possible and it's well worth the effort. You can prep some of the dish in advance. I've included three layers of veg but you can simplify it by just using extra aubergines in place of the potatoes and/or courgettes. It's also worth making a couple of moussakas at once so you have one in the freezer for a rainy day.

600g (1lb 5oz) potatoes (optional)
butter, for greasing
1 teaspoon fresh thyme or ½ teaspoon dried thyme
4–5 tablespoons olive oil
3 aubergines
3 courgettes (optional)
1 onion, chopped
4 garlic cloves, crushed
800g (1lb 12oz) minced lamb (or use minced beef)
2 teaspoons dried oregano
1 teaspoon ground cumin
½ teaspoon ground cinnamon
2 tablespoons tomato purée
1 tablespoon Worcestershire sauce
100ml (3½fl oz) red wine
400g (14oz) can chopped tomatoes
salt and pepper
green salad or Green Bean Almondine (*see* page 180), to serve

Preheat the oven to 200°C Fan/220°C/425°F/ Gas Mark 7. Line 2 baking trays with nonstick baking paper.

Start by slicing the potatoes (if using) into 5mm (¼ inch) thick slices. Tip into a colander and rinse under the running cold tap. Dry with kitchen paper or a clean tea towel.

Grease a 30 x 20cm (12 x 8 inch) ovenproof dish with butter and lay the potato slices in the bottom so they overlap (they will shrink). Season with salt and pepper and sprinkle with thyme. Drizzle with 1 tablespoon of the olive oil and roast for 15 minutes. The potatoes won't be fully cooked, but you should be able to pierce them with a knife. You can skip this step if not using potatoes.

Trim the aubergines and courgettes (if using) and slice them lengthways into 5mm (¼ inch) thick slices. Lay the sliced vegetables on the lined baking trays in a single layer, sprinkle with thyme then drizzle with 3 tablespoons of the olive oil and season well. Bake the courgettes for 10 minutes and the aubergines for 15 minutes alongside the potatoes (if using). Alternatively, you can heat the oil in a large frying pan and sear the aubergine and courgette slices on both sides in batches on a high heat. Once roasted/ seared, set the veg aside for now.

Meanwhile, heat the remaining 1 tablespoon of olive oil in a large, ovenproof pan and add the onion and garlic. Cook on a medium heat for 5 minutes before adding the minced lamb. Cook until all the meat has changed colour, breaking it up with a wooden spoon as it cooks.

Recipe continued overleaf →

FOR THE BÉCHAMEL SAUCE
40g (1½oz) butter
3 tablespoons plain flour
400–450ml (14–16fl oz) milk
50g (1¾oz) Parmesan cheese, grated, plus extra for finishing
¼ teaspoon grated nutmeg
2 eggs

TIPS
The cooked lamb mixture is ideal for making ahead and it freezes well. Cool the cooked lamb mixture, then transfer to an airtight container and refrigerate for up to 3 days, or freeze for up to 3 months (defrost before assembling the moussaka as above).

The assembled unbaked or fully baked moussaka is also ideal for batch cooking and making ahead and it freezes well. Cool the baked moussaka in the dish (no need to cool if unbaked), then cover the moussaka tightly with tin foil and freeze for up to 3 months (defrost before baking as above or reheating to serve).

Add the oregano, cumin, cinnamon, tomato purée and Worcestershire sauce to the minced lamb followed by the wine. Stir and let it bubble for a few minutes, then add the tomatoes.

Bring to a simmer, then cook on a low heat for 45 minutes or cover and cook in the oven at 140°C Fan/160°C/325°F/Gas Mark 3, for 2 hours. Alternatively, transfer the simmering mixture to a slow cooker, cover and cook on medium for 4 hours or on low for 7 hours.

Remove the pan from the heat and set aside while you make the béchamel sauce. You can refrigerate or freeze the lamb mixture at this point too for another day (*see* Tips below).

Preheat the oven to 180°C Fan/200°C/400°F/ Gas Mark 6.

Make the (all-in-one method) béchamel sauce. Add the butter, flour and milk to a saucepan. Cook on a medium heat, whisking all the time, until you have a smooth, thick sauce.

Stir in the grated cheese and nutmeg then set aside to cool for 10 minutes (or the eggs will scramble). Whisk in the eggs.

To assemble the moussaka, add half the aubergine slices on top of the potatoes (if using) or place in the prepared ovenproof dish, followed by half the courgette slices (if using), then the meat sauce. Repeat with the remaining aubergines and courgettes (if using).

Pour over the béchamel sauce, then grate over more Parmesan. Bake the moussaka for 40 minutes, or until the top is golden brown and bubbling.

Serve with a green salad or Green Beans Almondine.

Prep time: 20 minutes | **Cooking time:** 4½–5½ hours, or 8 hours or overnight | **Serves:** 6–8

Smoky Beef Brisket with Coleslaw

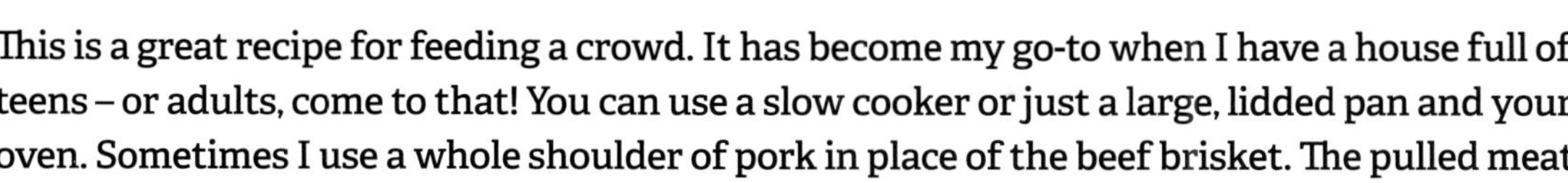

This is a great recipe for feeding a crowd. It has become my go-to when I have a house full of teens – or adults, come to that! You can use a slow cooker or just a large, lidded pan and your oven. Sometimes I use a whole shoulder of pork in place of the beef brisket. The pulled meat can be served with salad and potatoes, or loaded into buns with the coleslaw.

2 onions, each cut into 3 discs
2kg (4lb 8oz) piece of beef brisket

FOR THE RUB
1 tablespoon smoked paprika
2 tablespoons brown sugar
2 teaspoons ground cumin
2 teaspoons salt
2 teaspoons garlic granules
½ teaspoon pepper
1 teaspoon English mustard

FOR THE SAUCE
2 garlic cloves, crushed
5 tablespoons tomato ketchup
2 tablespoons Worcestershire sauce
3 tablespoons apple cider vinegar
juice of 1 clementine
½ teaspoon cayenne pepper
1 teaspoon salt

Combine all the rub ingredients in a bowl. Mix all the sauce ingredients together in a jug.

Put the onion discs in the bottom of the slow cooker or large lidded flameproof casserole dish. If the brisket is rolled, remove the string and unroll. Spread the rub all over, then lay the brisket on the onions.

Pour over the sauce, making sure the meat is coated, pop the lid on the slow cooker and cook on high for 6 hours or on low for 12 hours or overnight. Alternatively, if cooking in a conventional oven, preheat the oven to 180°C Fan/200°C/400°F/Gas Mark 6.

Put a lid on the casserole dish and cook in the oven for 30 minutes, then turn the temperature down to 130°C Fan/150°C/300°F/Gas Mark 2 and cook for a further 4–5 hours, until the meat is very tender.

When it's ready, carefully lift out the brisket on to a plate and keep hot. Either pour the juices into a small pan (if using a slow cooker) or transfer the casserole to the hob and reduce the juices by half on a high heat. Ideally pour the juices into a separating jug. Alternatively, pour them into a jug, leave to stand for 10 minutes and let the juices separate from the fat, then discard the fat from the top.

Recipe continued overleaf →

Continued

FOR THE COLESLAW
3 tablespoons apple cider vinegar
1 red onion, finely sliced
100g (3½oz) Greek yogurt
1 tablespoon Dijon mustard
1 teaspoon salt
1 sweetheart (hispi) cabbage, cored and finely shredded
2 large carrots, grated

TO SERVE
6–8 seeded brioche burger buns
Potato Salad (*see* page 177)

Pull the brisket apart into shreds with two forks then mix with the reduced pan juices.

To make the coleslaw, combine 2 tablespoons of the vinegar with the red onion in a small bowl. Leave to sit for 15 minutes, then pour the vinegar away. Whisk the yogurt together with the Dijon mustard, salt and the remaining vinegar in a large bowl. Combine the cabbage, red onion and carrots with the yogurt mixture.

Serve the pulled beef brisket and pan juices with the coleslaw. Pile the brisket and coleslaw into burger buns and serve with potato salad alongside.

ADAPTATIONS
- Follow the same recipe for a whole shoulder of pork.
- For gluten-free, use gluten-free mustards, gluten-free Worcestershire sauce and gluten-free burger buns.

TIPS
If batch cooking, double the quantities. The brisket will keep in the refrigerator for up to 3 days in an airtight container. It can be reheated in a pan or covered in foil in the oven for 30 minutes at 170°C Fan/190°C/375°F/Gas Mark 5.

The brisket can be frozen in its sauce for up to 3 months. Defrost before reheating as above.

The coleslaw can be made ahead and also batch made. It will keep in the refrigerator in an airtight container for up to 3 days.

Prep time: 10 minutes | **Cooking time:** 40 minutes | **Serves:** 6

Salmon & Tzatziki Platter

Some of the best recipes are discovered by accident. This is one of them, inspired when I paired some grilled salmon with a side of Greek salad. The flavours went so well together that I decided to combine the two into a sharing platter. Feel free to use individual salmon fillets or a whole side of salmon.

4 tablespoons olive oil
finely grated zest and juice of 1 lemon
3 garlic cloves, crushed
1 tablespoon dried oregano
1 tablespoon Dijon mustard
2 tablespoons red or white wine vinegar
1kg (2lb 4oz) new potatoes, scrubbed and halved
300g (10½oz) cherry tomatoes
1 red onion, sliced
150g (5½oz) pitted black olives
1kg (2lb 4oz) side of salmon or 6 individual salmon fillets
100g (3½oz) feta cheese, cubed
salt and pepper

FOR THE TZATZIKI
1 cucumber
100g (3½oz) Greek yogurt
juice of 1 lemon
1 teaspoon salt

TO SERVE
basil leaves
green salad leaves

Preheat the oven to 180°C Fan/200°C/400°F/ Gas Mark 6.

In a bowl, mix 2 tablespoons of the olive oil with the lemon zest and juice, the garlic, oregano, mustard and vinegar to make a dressing. Set aside.

Add the potatoes to a large roasting tray. Season well with salt and pepper, then drizzle with the remaining 2 tablespoons of olive oil.

Roast the potatoes for 15 minutes. Toss through the cherry tomatoes, red onion and black olives.

If using individual salmon fillets, return the roasting tray to the oven for another 15 minutes before adding the salmon. Spoon the dressing over the salmon fillets and potatoes, then roast for 10 minutes more, or until the salmon flakes easily and the potatoes are cooked.

If using a whole salmon side, add it to the middle of the roasting tray once the potatoes have had 15 minutes in the oven. Spoon the dressing over the salmon and potatoes. Return to the oven for 25 minutes, or until the salmon flakes easily and the potatoes are cooked.

Meanwhile, for the tzatziki, coarsely grate the cucumber and squeeze out the excess water. Combine the cucumber with the other ingredients in a bowl, then set aside.

Scatter the crumbled feta scattered over the traybake and garnish with basil leaves. Serve with the tzatziki on the side and some green salad leaves.

ADAPTATION

▸ For gluten-free, use gluten-free Dijon mustard.

Prep time: 30 minutes | **Cooking time:** 1½ hours | **Serves:** 6

Tapas

A Spanish-style tapas feast is one of my favourite ways to feed friends. I developed a real love of proper tapas food when I visited San Sebastián many years ago. This is my take on my favourite dishes, with something for everyone.

FOR THE PATATAS BRAVAS
1kg (2lb 4oz) potatoes, cut into 3–4cm (1¼–1½ inch) chunks (no need to peel them)
2 teaspoon smoked paprika
5 tablespoons olive oil
1 onion, chopped
3 garlic cloves, crushed
1 tablespoon balsamic vinegar
400g (14oz) can chopped tomatoes
½–1 teaspoon chilli flakes
salt and pepper

FOR THE CROQUETTES
800g (1lb 12oz) potatoes, cubed
2 eggs
1 teaspoon salt
½ teaspoon pepper
120g (4¼oz) Cheddar cheese, grated
30g (1oz) jalapeños from a jar, finely chopped (optional)
30g g (1oz) ham, finely chopped (optional)
80g (2¾oz) any breadcrumbs or panko crumbs
spray oil (optional)

FOR THE CHORIZO IN RED WINE
300g (10½oz) cooking chorizo sausage, cut into 3cm (1¼ inch) slices
75ml (2½fl oz) red wine

FOR THE PIL PIL PRAWNS
4 tablespoons olive oil
4 garlic cloves, sliced
24 large raw peeled prawns, defrosted if frozen
¼ teaspoon smoked paprika
¼ teaspoon chilli flakes
1 tablespoon chopped parsley

FOR THE GARLIC MUSHROOMS
1 tablespoon olive oil
15g (½oz) butter
2 garlic cloves, crushed
300g (10½oz) button mushrooms, trimmed
2 tablespoons white wine or dry sherry (optional)
1 tablespoon chopped parsley
salt and pepper

FOR THE SPINACH
2 tablespoons pine nuts (optional)
200g (7oz) fresh spinach, chopped
salt and pepper

FOR THE PADRÓN PEPPERS
260g (9½oz) Padrón peppers
1 teaspoon coarse sea salt, plus extra to serve

TO SERVE
pitted olives (black and/or green)
sliced Manchego cheese drizzled with honey
sliced Spanish cooked meats
fresh crusty bread

ADAPTATIONS

- All recipes expect the croquettes, chorizo and prawns are vegetarian. To make the croquettes vegetarian, omit the ham.
- All recipes except the croquettes and garlic mushrooms are dairy-free. To make the garlic mushrooms dairy-free, use an extra tablespoon of oil instead of the butter.
- All recipes except the croquettes are gluten-free. Use gluten-free breadcrumbs to make the croquettes gluten-free.

FOR THE PATATAS BRAVAS
Preheat the oven to 180°C Fan/200°C/400°F/Gas Mark 6. Line a baking sheet with nonstick baking paper.

Cook the potatoes in a pan of salted boiling water for 4 minutes, then drain and shake a little to fluff up the edges. Tip on to the lined baking sheet. Season with salt and pepper, sprinkle with 1 teaspoon smoked paprika and drizzle with 4 tablespoons of the olive oil. Roast for 40 minutes, or until golden and crispy.

Meanwhile, soften the onion in the remaining olive oil in a pan on a medium heat for 5 minutes. Add all the remaining ingredients, bring to a simmer and cook for 20 minutes. Spoon the warm spicy tomato sauce over the roasted potatoes to serve.

FOR THE CROQUETTES
Preheat the oven to 180°C Fan/200°C/400°F/Gas Mark 6. Line a baking sheet with nonstick baking paper.

Cook the potatoes in a pan of salted boiling water for 15 minutes, or until you can easily insert a knife into the middle. Drain, then roughly mash the potatoes and allow to cool slightly. Add 1 beaten egg to the potatoes along with the salt, pepper and Cheddar. You can also add the jalapeños and ham now if using. Mash again to combine.

Beat the remaining egg in a bowl. Pour the breadcrumbs on to a plate. Using your hands, form the potato mixture into 12 balls, each a little bigger than a golf ball. Roll each ball in the beaten egg, then in the breadcrumbs to coat.

Place close together on the lined baking sheet and bake in the oven for 25 minutes, or cook in a preheated air fryer at 195°C/380°F for 15 minutes, until golden and crispy. For both methods, you can spray the croquettes before and during cooking with oil, if you like, so they have extra crunch. Turn the croquettes over a couple or so times during cooking. Serve hot.

FOR THE CHORIZO IN RED WINE
Preheat the oven to 180°C Fan/200°C/400°F/Gas Mark 6 or the air fryer to 190°C/375°F. Add the chorizo slices to an ovenproof dish, then pour over the red wine. Cook in the oven for 20 minutes, or in the air fryer for 12 minutes, until dark in colour. Serve hot.

FOR THE PIL PIL PRAWNS
Heat the olive oil in a pan until hot, then add the garlic and prawns. Cook on a medium heat for 2 minutes, then add the smoked paprika and chilli flakes. Cook for another 2 minutes until the prawns are pink. Serve with the parsley sprinkled over.

FOR THE GARLIC MUSHROOMS
Heat the olive oil and butter in a pan until hot. Add the garlic and mushrooms, season with salt and pepper, then cook on a medium heat for 2 minutes. Add the wine or sherry (if using) and cook for another 5 minutes. Serve with the parsley sprinkled over.

FOR THE SPINACH
Dry roast the pine nuts (if using) on a low heat for 2–3 minutes. Add the spinach to the same pan you cooked the mushrooms in along with some seasoning. Let the spinach wilt for 1–2 minutes, adding a splash of water if needed. Top with the toasted pine nuts then serve.

FOR THE PADRÓN PEPPERS
Heat a large pan until hot. Add the Padrón peppers and salt. Cook on a high heat for 3 minutes until charred and blistering, turning them regularly. Sprinkle with extra salt to serve.

Serve all your tapas dishes with plates/bowls of pitted olives, sliced Manchego cheese drizzled with honey, sliced Spanish cooked meats and fresh crusty bread to accompany.

Prep time: 20 minutes, plus chilling | **Cooking time:** 1 hour 5 minutes | **Serves:** 4

Baked Meatballs Two Ways

These are my ultimate meatballs! Making them larger in size and oven-baking them means they're crisp on the outside and meltingly tender on the inside.

olive oil, for frying the meatballs
basil leaves, to garnish
crusty bread or pasta, to serve

FOR VEGETARIAN MEATBALLS
100g (3½oz) fresh spinach
250g (9oz) cooked lentils of your choice
1 small onion, grated
1 small carrot, grated
2 garlic cloves, crushed
50g (1¾oz) panko crumbs or any breadcrumbs
1 tablespoon balsamic vinegar
3 tablespoons grated vegetarian/vegan hard cheese, plus 2 tablespoons extra for sprinkling
½ teaspoon salt and a generous few grinds of pepper
1 teaspoon each paprika, ground coriander, dried oregano
1 egg, whisked
150g (5¼oz) mozzarella cheese, drained and cut into 1.5cm (⅝ inch) cubes

FOR BEEF MEATBALLS
800g (1lb 12oz) minced beef
1 small onion, grated
1 tablespoon dried oregano
1 egg, whisked
1 carrot, grated
60g (2¼oz) panko crumbs
25g (1oz) Parmesan cheese, grated, plus 2 tablespoons extra for sprinkling
½ teaspoon salt and a generous few grinds of pepper
150g (5¼oz) mozzarella cheese, drained and cut into 1.5cm (⅝ inch) cubes

FOR THE TOMATO SAUCE
1 tablespoon olive oil
2 onions, chopped
3 garlic cloves, crushed
2 tablespoons balsamic vinegar
2 x 400g (14oz) cans chopped tomatoes
100ml (3½fl oz) red wine
2 bay leaves
½ teaspoon sea salt flakes

For the veggie meatballs, put the spinach into a colander and pour over boiling water to wilt it. Squeeze out the excess water and finely chop.

Whether making meat or vegetarian meatballs, combine all the meatball ingredients, apart from the mozzarella, in a large bowl, then using your hands, divide and shape the mixture into 12 equal balls, adding a cube of mozzarella into the middle of each one as you go. Each meatball should be about 6cm (2½ inch) diameter. You will only use half the cheese – the rest is used later. Place on a plate and refrigerate for at least 10 minutes.

Preheat the oven to 180°C Fan/200°C/400°F/ Gas Mark 6.

Make the tomato sauce. Heat the olive oil in a flameproof casserole dish, then soften the onions and garlic on a medium heat for 5 minutes. Add all the remaining sauce ingredients, then bring to a simmer and cook for 10 minutes.

Meanwhile, heat a splash of olive oil in a nonstick frying pan and colour the meatballs on a high heat for 5 minutes. You can do this in batches, if needed.

Nestle the meatballs into the tomato sauce, then cover and bake for 30 minutes. Uncover, sprinkle over the extra Parmesan or vegetarian/vegan cheese and remaining mozzarella and bake for another 15 minutes. The cheese should be bubbling, the meatballs dark in colour and the sauce rich.

Finish with basil leaves and serve with crusty bread or pasta.

TIP
This can be frozen for up to 3 months if you want to batch cook it.

Prep time: 10 minutes, plus marinating | **Cooking time:** 10 minutes | **Serves:** 6

Burrata, Nectarine & Giant Crouton Salad

Burrata makes a regular appearance on our summer menu. It takes on marinades so well and this basil burrata pairs beautifully with sweet fruits such as nectarines. I like to serve it as a platter, with giant croutons and Parma ham, but you can also load the burrata, Parma ham and nectarines on to toasted slices of bread to make an alternative to traditional bruschetta. You can substitute the nectarines for peaches, tomatoes, figs or apricots, if you prefer.

2 x 150g (5½oz) burrata balls, drained
finely grated zest and juice of 1 lemon
250g (9oz) ciabatta or sourdough loaf, sliced or roughly torn
1 teaspoon salt
2 tablespoons extra virgin olive oil
1 garlic clove
4–6 ripe but firm nectarines, pitted and cut into wedges (or use peaches, 500g/1lb 2oz mixed tomatoes, quartered figs or apricots)
200g (7oz) Parma ham or prosciutto slices

FOR THE BASIL OIL
30g (1oz) basil, leaves only
½ teaspoon salt
100ml (3½fl oz) extra virgin olive oil

Blitz together all the ingredients for the basil oil in a blender or food processor. You can also use a pestle and mortar to do this.

Sit the burrata balls in a bowl. Finely grate over the lemon zest and squeeze over the lemon juice. Pour over half the basil oil. Leave to marinate at room temperature for 20 minutes.

Preheat the oven to 180°C Fan/200°C/400°F/ Gas Mark 6.

Place the bread on a nonstick baking tray, sprinkle over the salt and drizzle with the olive oil. Bake for 10 minutes, or until golden and crisp. Swipe each piece of crisp bread twice with the garlic clove.

Arrange everything on a platter, drizzling the juices from the marinated burrata over the top and finishing with the remaining basil oil.

ADAPTATION

- Serve the Parma ham or prosciutto on the side if you have vegetarian guests, and make sure you use vegetarian burrata.

Prep time: 10 minutes | **Cooking time:** 35 minutes | **Serves:** 4

Saffron & Prawn Risotto

This is a delicious, weekend-worthy risotto. I love making risottos but these days they are definitely only a weekend order. I find the standing and stirring process quite cathartic and it gives me an excuse not to move from my spot! For the best result, source the plumpest juiciest king prawns you can – their flavour is so much better than the tiny prawns you often find.

20–24 raw shell-on or peeled king prawns, defrosted if frozen
1 litre (1¾ pints) fish or veg stock
1 tablespoon olive oil
1 onion, finely chopped
3 garlic cloves, crushed
300g (10½oz) Arborio/risotto rice
large pinch of saffron threads (¼ teaspoon)
100ml (3½fl oz) white wine
3 fresh tomatoes, chopped
50g (1¾oz) fresh spinach, chopped, or frozen peas or edamame
juice of 1 lemon
salt and pepper
grated Parmesan cheese, to serve

TIP

You don't have to use shell-on prawns but if you buy these, adding the shells to the stock while it simmers will add an extra depth of flavour.

ADAPTATIONS

- This saffron risotto makes a great vegan meal if you omit the prawns, use veg stock, sub the wine with extra stock (if preferred) and add 200g (7oz) extra fresh veg. Chopped green beans all work well. Swap the Parmesan for a hard vegan cheese.
- For dairy-free, simply omit the Parmesan and use a hard vegan cheese instead.
- For gluten-free, use a gluten-free stock cube or bouillon powder, or use homemade fish/veg stock.

If you have shell-on prawns, remove the shells (set the prawns aside), put them in a pan and cover with the stock. Bring to a simmer and cook for a few minutes, then strain the stock to remove the shells and transfer back to the pan. Keep the stock simmering on a low heat. If using peeled prawns, simply heat your stock in a pan and keep it simmering on a low heat.

Heat the olive oil in a separate deep pan, add the onion and cook on a medium heat for about 5 minutes. Add the garlic, colour for a minute, then add the rice. Stir and add the saffron threads.

Pour in the wine, let it reduce on a high heat, then add the hot stock, one ladleful at a time. Keep stirring, adding another ladleful of the stock as soon as the rice has absorbed the previous ladleful.

Once half the stock has been added, stir in the tomatoes, then go back to adding the remaining stock a ladleful at a time, as before.

After 25 minutes, the risotto should be pretty much cooked. Try some – the rice should be firm but not crunchy. Add the prawns and the frozen peas/edamame (if using) and give the pan a stir again, then cook gently for a further 6 minutes, or until the prawns have turned pink.

Add the chopped spinach (if using), squeeze in the lemon juice, check for seasoning, adding a little salt and pepper, if needed, then serve with grated Parmesan sprinkled over.

Prep time: 15 minutes | Cooking time: 3 hours 40 minutes–8 hours | Serves: 6

Asian-style Pulled Pork

This is always a crowd-pleaser. I have suggested serving the juicy, shredded meat with pancakes or wraps, spring onions, cucumber and my homemade Hoisin Sauce (*see* page 20), but it is also delicious served as a stew with rice and veg.

2kg (4lb 8oz) boneless pork shoulder joint, or use 2kg (4lb 8oz) beef short ribs
1 teaspoon Chinese five spice
1 tablespoon olive oil
salt and pepper

FOR THE STOCK
1 litre (1¾ pints) chicken stock
6 star anise
1 cinnamon stick
1 teaspoon Sichuan peppercorns, crushed
5cm (2 inch) piece of fresh root ginger, finely chopped
3 garlic cloves, crushed
3 tablespoons brown sugar
75ml (2½fl oz) soy sauce
75ml (2½fl oz) mirin (rice wine), or sub with white wine
juice of ½ small orange or 1 clementine, or 3 tablespoons orange juice

TO SERVE
Asian pancakes or tortilla wraps
Hoisin Sauce (*see* page 20)
1 cucumber, cut into batons
bunch of spring onions, trimmed and shredded

TIPS

The pork shoulder can be cooked ahead and cooled, then covered and left in the refrigerator for up to 3 days. Reheat thoroughly covered in foil in the oven.

Leftover stock can be cooled and will keep in an airtight container in the refrigerator for up to 3 days, or frozen for up to 3 months (defrost before reheating). Add cooked noodles to any leftover stock (or cook some noodles in the stock), with some vegetables and any leftover pork or cooked chicken, for a delicious noodle soup later in the week.

Preheat the oven to 140°C Fan/160°C/325°F/Gas Mark 3 unless using a slow cooker (*see* below).

Season the pork joint or beef ribs with salt and pepper, then sprinkle over the Chinese five spice.

Heat the oil in a large flameproof casserole pan and colour the joint or ribs on all sides on a high heat. You might need to colour the ribs in batches. Set aside on a plate and discard any oil from the pan.

Add all the stock ingredients to the pan and bring to a simmer. Add the joint or ribs to the stock, cover then transfer the pan to the oven and cook for 3½ hours, or until the meat can be pulled apart with a fork. The rib meat should be falling off the bones.

Ideally pour the juices from the pan into a separating jug. Alternatively, pour the juices into a jug, leave to stand for 10 minutes and let the juices separate from the fat, then discard the fat from the top.

Gently shred the pork with two forks. The beef ribs can be served whole. Serve with Asian pancakes or tortilla wraps, hoisin sauce, cucumber batons and spring onions for everyone to help themselves. I like to serve the meat on a platter with some of the juices poured over the top and the rest in a jug. There will be excess juices left over (*see* Tips).

Slow cooker method: Season the pork joint or beef ribs with salt and pepper, then sprinkle over the Chinese five spice. Colour in a pan on a high heat for 2 minutes on each side before transferring to a slow cooker pan. Add the remaining ingredients, then cook on low for 8 hours or on high for 5 hours.

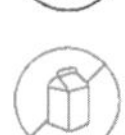

Prep time: 10 minutes | **Cooking time:** 55 minutes | **Serves:** 4

Spiced Chicken, Cauliflower & Lentil Traybake

One of my favourite vegetarian dishes is tarka dhal and I would happily eat a bowl of it for dinner. However, my boys require a bit more filling up and so I set to work on creating a dhal-inspired traybake that included chicken. Cauliflower florets mean there's no need to cook a separate vegetable on the side. The traybake is finished with a buttery garlic and cumin drizzle (like a tarka). In place of the cauliflower you could use potatoes, squash or aubergine.

1 tablespoon olive or groundnut oil
8 skin-on, bone-in chicken portions or 4 chicken breasts approx. 150g (5½oz) each
2 onions, chopped
4 garlic cloves, chopped
2 teaspoons garam masala
1 teaspoon ground turmeric
2 teaspoons ground cumin
2 teaspoons ground coriander
1 teaspoon salt
250g (9oz) dried red lentils
10cm (4 inch) piece of fresh root ginger, finely chopped
5 plum tomatoes, quartered
700ml (1¼ pints) veg or chicken stock
1–2 red chillies, finely chopped
1 cauliflower, split into florets

FOR THE TARKA
30g (1oz) butter
1 tablespoon groundnut or vegetable oil
1 teaspoon cumin seeds
3 garlic cloves, slice

Preheat the oven to 180°C Fan/200°C/400°F/ Gas Mark 6.

Heat a flameproof roasting tin on the hob until hot, then add the oil and chicken, skin-side down, to the tin and colour on a high heat for 5 minutes. Transfer the chicken to a plate and set aside.

Add the onions and garlic to the tin and colour for a couple of minutes before adding the spices then all the remaining ingredients, apart from the cauliflower florets. Bring to a simmer.

Return the chicken to the tin, making sure the chicken skin sits above the sauce, then transfer to the oven and cook for 30 minutes.

Add the cauliflower florets to the tin, turning them over in the sauce, then return the tin to the oven and cook for a further 15 minutes until tender.

Just before serving, make the tarka. Melt the butter and oil in a small pan on a medium heat. Add the cumin seeds and garlic slices and cook for 1 minute. Drizzle the tarka over the cooked traybake and serve.

TIP

This traybake is great for batch cooking and it freezes well (without the tarka – make this fresh when you come to serve the dish). Cool the cooked traybake and transfer to an airtight container, then freeze for up to 3 months. Defrost before reheating to serve.

ADAPTATIONS

- For gluten-free, use a gluten-free stock cube or bouillon powder, or use homemade veg or chicken stock (*see* Tip on page 49 to make my homemade chicken stock).
- For dairy-free, omit the butter from the tarka and use 3 tablespoons of oil instead.

Prep time: 20 minutes | **Cooking time:** 2 hours 10 minutes–6¾ hours | **Serves:** 6

Glazed Ham

Not just for Christmas, a whole cooked gammon is a great Sunday lunch centrepiece. It can be sliced and kept in the refrigerator (it will keep in an airtight container for up to 3 days) for lunches and dinners. I've provided a few ideas for different glazes for you to try.

2kg (4lb 8oz) whole gammon joint, boneless, unsmoked
1 onion, quartered
2 carrots, roughly chopped
1 clementine, halved
2 bay leaves
2 sprigs of rosemary
1 teaspoon black peppercorns
4 whole cloves

FOR APRICOT & BRANDY GLAZE
4 tablespoons apricot jam
2 tablespoons brown sugar
2 tablespoons wholegrain mustard
1 tablespoon brandy

FOR HONEY & CLEMENTINE GLAZE
4 tablespoons honey
2 tablespoons brown sugar
juice of ½ clementine or ½ small orange
1 tablespoon Dijon mustard

FOR POMEGRANATE & ORANGE GLAZE
4 tablespoons pomegranate molasses
2 tablespoons brown sugar
juice of ½ orange

TO SERVE
Maple-roasted Root Vegetables (*see* page 175)
ready-made parsley sauce

TIPS

Once the ham has been poached in the stock (which you can use in soups), it can be cooled, covered tightly and refrigerated for up to 2 days before glazing.

The fully cooked (cold) ham can also be frozen. Slice or chop the cold ham, transfer to an airtight container and freeze for up to 3 months. Defrost in the refrigerator overnight before using.

Put the gammon and the other ingredients in a flameproof casserole pan or slow cooker. Pour in 2 litres (3½ pints) of water so it nearly comes to the top of the gammon. If cooking on the hob, bring it slowly to the boil, then reduce the heat, cover and simmer for 1¼ hours. Or cook in a slow cooker on low for 6 hours.

Leave the ham in the stock to cool slightly, then lift it out, discarding any string. Remove the rind, leaving a layer of fat on the ham. Score the fat at 1cm (½ inch) intervals in a criss-cross pattern.

Combine your chosen glaze ingredients in a small pan and heat gently, stirring, until the sugar dissolves.

If oven-baking, preheat the oven to 190°C Fan/210°C/410°F/Gas Mark 6½. Line a baking tray with nonstick baking paper. Sit the ham on the lined tray. Brush the ham all over with half the glaze, and bake for 20 minutes, then brush with the remaining glaze and bake for a further 20 minutes until golden.

Leave to rest for 15 minutes before carving then serve hot with the Maple-roasted Root Vegetables and parsley sauce.

Air fryer method: Loosely wrap the uncooked gammon joint in foil and cook in a preheated air fryer at 170°C/340°F for 1½ hours. If you have a smaller air fryer, a 1.5kg (3lb 5oz) joint will take 1 hour 10 minutes to cook, a 1kg (2lb 4oz) joint 50 minutes or a 500g (1lb 2oz) joint 25 minutes.

To glaze, uncover, then remove the rind and score the fat. Return the ham directly in the basket, brush over half the glaze and cook for 10 minutes, then brush over the remaining glaze and cook for a further 10 minutes until golden. Serve as above.

ADAPTATION

- For gluten-free, use gluten-free mustards.

Prep time: 10 minutes | **Cooking time:** 25 minutes | **Serves:** 6

Tartiflette

I love this Alpine classic so much that the recipe had to feature in this chapter. I know I talk a lot about simplifying recipes and looking for healthier options, but there are times when you just have to hold your hands up and appreciate that the soul of a dish relies on wondrously rich ingredients and you shouldn't mess with it! So, here's an indulgent meal full of cheese, bacon, potatoes, wine and cream.

800g (1lb 12oz) waxy potatoes, sliced
splash of olive oil
250g (9oz) bacon lardons
1 onion, finely chopped
1 garlic clove, crushed
100ml (3½fl oz) white wine
400g (14oz) Reblochon cheese, quartered
200ml (7fl oz) double cream
salt and pepper

TO SERVE
thyme leaves
cornichons
side salad
crusty bread (optional)
cooked steaks (optional)

Preheat the oven to 190°C Fan/210°C/410°F/ Gas Mark 6½.

Start by cooking the potatoes in a pan of lightly salted boiling water for 4 minutes until soft but not falling apart. Drain and set aside.

Heat a large ovenproof frying pan until hot, then add the splash of olive oil, the bacon lardons and onion. Colour on a medium heat for 5 minutes, then add the garlic and cook for 1 minute more. Pour in the wine and cook for a further minute.

Tip in the potatoes, season with salt and pepper and stir. Take the pan off the heat and add the cheese slices followed by the cream.

Bake for 12–15 minutes until the cheese has melted and the tartiflette is golden brown.

Finish with thyme leaves, then serve with cornichons and a side salad. This is also lovely with crusty bread and/or cooked steaks.

TIP

If you can't source Reblochon (it is a seasonal cheese mostly available from November to February), you can substitute it with Brie.

ADAPTATION

- For a vegetarian version, omit the bacon lardons and replace the Reblochon with Brie. Serve with bread and/or a side salad.

Prep time: 15 minutes | **Cooking time:** 3¼–8¼ hours | **Serves:** 6

Lamb Shank Tagine

This is a true one-pot wonder which you can prep in advance, pop in a low oven or slow cooker and then forget about for several hours – perfect for serving to friends for dinner or on a lazy Sunday.

6 lamb shanks, approx. 300g (10½oz) each; or use 1kg/2lb 4oz diced lamb neck fillet or shoulder
1 tablespoon olive oil
2 onions, chopped
3 garlic cloves, crushed
5cm (2 inch) piece of fresh root ginger, peeled and chopped (or use 1 tablespoon ginger paste)
2 teaspoons ground cumin
2 teaspoons ground coriander
1 teaspoon ground cinnamon (or 1 cinnamon stick)
1 bay leaf
200g (7oz) fresh tomatoes, roughly chopped, or ½ x 400g (14oz) can chopped tomatoes
350g (12oz) dried green or Puy lentils, rinsed
1 litre (1¾ pints) chicken or lamb stock
400g (14oz) butternut squash flesh (peeled and deseeded weight), cubed
2 preserved lemons, chopped, or finely grated zest and juice of 1 fresh lemon
100g (3½oz) dried cherries (or swap for chopped dried apricots)
salt and pepper

TO SERVE
cooked couscous, mashed potatoes or Couscous Salad (*see* page 173)
2 tablespoons flaked almonds
50g (1¾oz) feta cheese, crumbled (optional)
2 tablespoons chopped fresh coriander
Green Beans Almondine (*see* page 180) (optional)

Take the lamb shanks out of the refrigerator and remove their packaging at least 30 minutes before preparing. Season the shanks with salt and pepper.

If cooking in the oven, preheat the oven to 140°C Fan/160°C/325°F/Gas Mark 3.

Whether using the oven or slow cooker, start by heating the olive oil in a large, flameproof casserole pan until hot. Add the shanks and colour on a high heat for 10–15 minutes until browned all over. Remove the shanks from the casserole pan.

Add the onions and garlic and cook for 2 minutes before adding the ginger, spices, bay leaf, tomatoes, lentils and stock. Return the shanks to the pan.

If cooking in the oven, bring to a simmer, then put a lid on the pan, transfer to the oven and cook for 3 hours, adding the squash, preserved lemons or lemon zest and juice and the dried cherries for the final 40 minutes.

If using a slow cooker, transfer tagine from the pan to a slow cooker. Cover and cook on low for 8 hours, adding the squash, preserved lemons or lemon zest and juice and the dried cherries for the final 1½ hours.

Once ready, the meat should be very tender and falling off the bones.

Serve the lamb shanks on top of couscous, mashed potatoes or my couscous salad, topped with the toasted almonds, crumbled feta (if using) and chopped coriander. Serve with the green beans to accompany, if you like.

ADAPTATIONS
- For gluten-free, serve this with mashed potatoes.
- For dairy-free, omit the feta.

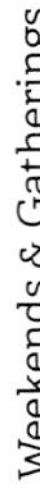

Prep time: 15 minutes | Cooking time: none | Serves: 4–6

Prawn & Mango Noodle Salad

This salad is so popular whenever I make it. When everyone dives in you can feel smug that it only took around 15 minutes to pull together.

500g (1lb 2oz) rice noodles, either dried or fresh
1 teaspoon sesame oil
500g (1lb 2oz) cooked peeled prawns
300g (10½oz) mangetout, each sliced into 3 (no need to cook them)
3 baby gem lettuce or ½ Chinese leaf cabbage, shredded
3 fresh ripe mangoes, pitted, peeled and sliced, or 300g (10½oz) ready-prepped mango flesh, sliced
handful of fresh mint and coriander leaves
1 red chilli, thinly sliced
100g (3½oz) toasted cashew nuts (optional)

FOR THE DRESSING
juice of 3 limes
2 tablespoons honey
3 tablespoons soy sauce or tamari
3 tablespoons olive oil
2 teaspoons sesame oil

Put the noodles in a heatproof bowl, cover with boiling water and leave to soak for dried noodles for 3 minutes, fresh noodles for 1 minute, or prepare according to the packet instructions.

Drain well, return to the bowl, then drizzle with the sesame oil and fork it through so the noodles don't stick together.

Shake/whisk all the dressing ingredients together in a clean jam jar or a small bowl.

Combine all the remaining ingredients and the prepped noodles in a serving bowl and toss together. Finish with the dressing and serve.

ADAPTATIONS

- Omit the prawns to keep the salad vegetarian. Some sliced raw sugar snaps are a great replacement. Or swap the prawns for cooked shredded chicken (use 4 cooked boneless, skinless chicken breasts).

Prep time: 15 minutes | **Cooking time:** 1¾ hours–5 hours 10 minutes | **Serves:** 4

Pot-roast Chicken & Chorizo Rice

I love the method of pot-roasting a chicken. It delivers the most tender meat possible and when you add rice to the pan it takes on all the flavour enhancers you choose to combine it with. I've given this pot roast a Spanish twist.

1 large onion, cut into 3 discs
1.8–2kg (4–4lb 8oz) whole chicken
3 teaspoons smoked paprika
2 tablespoons olive oil
1 lemon, halved
1 red pepper, cored, deseeded and chopped
2 garlic cloves, crushed
250g (9oz) cooking chorizo sausage, chopped
large pinch of saffron threads
1 tablespoon tomato purée
100ml (3½fl oz) white wine
250g (9oz) Bomba rice
800ml (28fl oz) chicken stock
100g (3½oz) frozen peas
salt and pepper
chopped parsley, to garnish

TIP

You can use your slow cooker for this recipe. Add all the ingredients to a slow cooker (ideally colour the onion discs and garlic in the oil first), including the rice and peas, and sit the chicken on top. Cover and cook on low for 5 hours until the chicken and rice are cooked. Fork through the rice to fluff it up. To crisp the skin, transfer the slow cooker pot (make sure it's ovenproof) to a preheated oven at 200°C Fan/220°C/425°F/ Gas Mark 7 for 10 minutes.

ADAPTATION

- For gluten-free, use a gluten-free stock cube or bouillon powder, or ideally use homemade stock (*see* Tip on page 49 to make my homemade chicken stock).

Preheat the oven to 180°C Fan/200°C/400°F/ Gas Mark 6.

Add the onion discs to a deep roasting tray or casserole dish and place the chicken on top.

Season the chicken well with salt and pepper, then sprinkle over 1 teaspoon of the smoked paprika. Drizzle with 1 tablespoon of the olive oil and rub all over the chicken.

Insert the lemon halves into the chicken cavity, cover with foil or the casserole lid and roast for 1 hour. Remove from the oven.

Heat the remaining olive oil in a pan until hot, then add the red pepper, garlic and chorizo and colour on a medium heat for 5 minutes. Add the remaining smoked paprika, the saffron, tomato purée and wine. Let the wine bubble for a minute, then stir in the rice. Spoon the rice mixture around the roast chicken and pour over the stock.

Re-cover and return the tray/dish to the oven and cook for a further 30 minutes, or until the chicken and rice are cooked (check the chicken is cooked by inserting the tip of a sharp knife into the thickest part of a thigh – the juices should run clear).

Take out of the oven and remove the foil/lid, then stir the peas through the rice. Turn the temperature up to 200°C Fan/220°C/425°F/Gas Mark 7 and return the uncovered tray/dish to the oven for a final 10 minutes to crisp the skin. Rest for 10 minutes.

Finish with some chopped parsley and take the pot-roast to the table to carve the chicken.

Prep time: 25 minutes | **Cooking time:** 40 minutes | **Serves:** 6

Harissa, Squash, Spinach & Feta Filo Tart

This is a fabulous vegetarian savoury pastry offering. It looks fancy but is actually very easy to make. It's just as good served cold as it is hot from the oven, so is great for lunch the next day too.

400g (14oz) fresh spinach, chopped
5 tablespoons rose harissa paste
3 tablespoons olive oil, plus extra for greasing
10 sheets of filo pastry (approx. 380g/13¼oz)
280g (10oz) sun-dried tomatoes, finely chopped
200g (7oz) feta cheese, crumbled
350g (12oz) butternut squash, peeled, deseeded and thinly sliced
4 eggs
200ml (7fl oz) double cream (or use a non-dairy alternative)
2 teaspoons thyme leaves
¼ teaspoon salt
few grinds of pepper

TIPS

This tart is great for batch cooking and making ahead. Prepare it up to the point of baking, then cover with clingfilm and place in the refrigerator for up to 6 hours. If making ahead and batch cooking, bake the tarts, let them cool then cover and keep in the refrigerator for up to 2 days. The tarts can be reheated in the oven. Cover with foil and bake at 160°C fan/180°C/350°F/Gas Mark 4 for 15 minutes.

Store any cold leftovers in an airtight container in the refrigerator for up to 3 days.

Preheat the oven to 180°C Fan/200°C/400°F/Gas Mark 6. Grease a 22 x 28cm (8½ x 11 inch) baking dish or tin with olive oil.

Put the fresh spinach in a colander and pour over boiling water to wilt it. Allow to cool, then squeeze out the water and roughly chop the spinach.

Mix together the rose harissa and the olive oil in a small bowl.

Work with one sheet of filo at a time. Leave the remaining filo covered with a damp tea towel so it doesn't dry out. Place a sheet of filo on a work surface or board and brush with the rose harissa and olive oil mixture.

Add some (about a tenth) of the chopped spinach and sun-dried tomatoes to the filo sheet, followed by some of the feta. Just dot everything randomly over the pastry sheet. It doesn't have to be perfect. Fold the pastry sheet widthways into 4cm (1½ inch) pleats, concertina fashion, and place in the prepared baking dish/tin lengthways.

Repeat with the remaining pastry sheets, harissa and olive oil mix, spinach, sun-dried tomatoes and feta. Stack the stuffed pastry pleats next to each other in the dish/tin as you go.

Slot the butternut squash slices in between the folds. Whisk together the eggs, cream, thyme, salt and pepper in a jug or bowl, then pour evenly over the tart.

Bake for 40 minutes, or until the pastry is golden and the eggs are set. Remove from the oven and leave the tart to sit for 10 minutes before slicing to serve.

Prep time: 10 minutes | **Cooking time:** 43 minutes | **Serves:** 6

Pesto Cod in Parma Ham Traybake

One-tray cooking at its best, this pesto cod wrapped in Parma ham has become one of my all-time favourite traybakes. It feels weekend worthy and is perfect for dinner parties, yet equally it's easy enough for a week night.

900g (2lb) Jersey Royal potatoes, scrubbed and halved
olive oil, for drizzling
6 slices of Parma ham
6 skinless cod loins, approx. 180g (6¼oz) each (or use hake or pollack)
6 tablespoons pesto (*see* page 92 to make your own), plus extra (optional) to serve
450g (1lb) asparagus spears, woody ends removed
300g (10½oz) cherry tomatoes
2 courgettes, sliced
juice of 1 lemon
salt and pepper
basil leaves, to garnish

Preheat the oven to 190°C Fan/210°C/410°F/ Gas Mark 6½.

Add the potatoes to a roasting tray with plenty of seasoning and drizzle generously with olive oil. Toss to coat, then roast for 25 minutes.

Meanwhile, top each slice of Parma ham with a cod loin. Season with salt and pepper, then spread 1 tablespoon of the pesto over each piece of fish. Wrap the Parma ham around the fish.

Take the part-roasted potatoes out of the oven and add the asparagus, cherry tomatoes and courgettes, then nestle in the ham-wrapped cod loins. Squeeze over the lemon juice and drizzle with olive oil.

Roast for a further 18 minutes, or until the fish is cooked and flakes easily with a fork, then finish with basil and serve with extra pesto drizzled over, if you like.

TIP

You can prep everything ahead, roasting the potatoes for the first 25 minutes, then allowing them to cool. Add the veg and the cod wrapped in Parma ham to the roasting tray, cover and refrigerate until needed. You can do this up to 24 hours ahead. Then simply squeeze over the lemon juice, drizzle with olive oil and bake as above.

Prep time: 15 minutes, plus marinating (optional) | **Cooking time:** 15–20 minutes | **Serves:** 6

Tandoori-style Chicken Salad

This is summer on a plate. Deliciously mild-spiced chicken which can be cooked on the barbecue, in the air fryer or on the hob, combined with new potatoes and salad, then finished with an Indian-inspired yogurt dressing. Any leftover salad can be kept in an airtight container in the refrigerator for a couple of days to serve for another meal.

1kg (2lb 4oz) boneless, skinless chicken breasts or thighs
500g (1lb 2oz) new potatoes, scrubbed and halved
100g (3½oz) salad leaves
1 cucumber, peeled into ribbons using a peeler
4 tablespoons pomegranate seeds, or 100g (3½oz) tomatoes, roughly chopped
2 tablespoons chopped fresh coriander, to garnish (optional)

FOR THE MARINADE
100g (3½oz) Greek yogurt
juice of 1 lemon
3 garlic cloves, crushed
2 teaspoons chopped fresh root ginger
1 teaspoon smoked paprika
1 teaspoon ground cumin
1 teaspoon ground coriander
1 teaspoon ground turmeric
1 teaspoon mild chilli powder
½ teaspoon salt

FOR THE YOGURT DRESSING
4 tablespoons Greek yogurt
3 tablespoons olive oil
juice of ½ lemon
½ teaspoon ground cumin
½ teaspoon ground coriander

ADAPTATION

- You can swap the chicken for raw peeled king prawns. Defrost if frozen and dry them before coating in the marinade. Cook in a hot griddle pan on the hob, on the barbecue, or under a preheated medium grill for about 6 minutes, turning over halfway through. Skewer them first and it'll make them easier to turn on the barbecue and under the grill. Alternatively, they will take 6 minutes to cook in a preheated air fryer at 190°C/375°F.

Combine all the marinade ingredients in a large mixing bowl.

If using chicken breasts, flatten them using a rolling pin between 2 sheets of nonstick baking paper, so they are 2cm (¾in) equal thickness. Add the chicken (flattened breasts or the thighs) to the marinade and turn to coat all over. Either cover and refrigerate for up to 24 hours before cooking, or they can be cooked straight away.

To cook the chicken, preheat a griddle pan on the hob until hot, then cook the chicken breasts on a medium heat for about 15 minutes, turning every couple of minutes, until fully cooked. Thighs will take about 20 minutes. Use the same timings for a barbecue, adding the chicken to a preheated barbecue on a medium heat.

If using an air fryer, preheat the air fryer to 190°C/375°F. Cook the chicken breasts for 12 minutes and the thighs for 18 minutes, turning the chicken halfway through the cooking time.

Meanwhile, cook the potatoes in a pan of salted boiling water for 12 minutes or until tender. Check they are cooked by piercing one in the middle with a knife. Drain.

Combine all the dressing ingredients in a jug or small bowl. Slice the cooked chicken once it's ready.

Arrange the salad leaves and cucumber ribbons on a platter, top with the potatoes, the chicken slices and the pomegranate seeds or tomatoes. Finally, spoon over the yogurt dressing and finish with the chopped coriander, then serve.

Prep time: 15 minutes | **Cooking time:** 4¼ hours–8 hours 10 minutes | **Serves:** 6

Slow-cooked Ox Cheeks in Red Wine

Ox cheeks are such an underrated cut of beef. They need to be slow cooked at a low temperature, so this dish is ideal for entertaining or prepping in advance. The result is beautifully tender, pull-apart meat in a deliciously rich sauce.

1.2kg (2lb 10oz) ox cheeks (or use shin or bavette (skirt) steak, but ideally have it in large whole pieces)
2 tablespoons plain flour
1 teaspoon salt
½ teaspoon pepper
1 bulb of garlic
1 tablespoon olive oil
15g (½oz) butter
2 onions, chopped
3 sprigs of rosemary, leaves picked and finely chopped
3 bay leaves
2 tablespoons tomato purée
300ml (10fl oz) beef stock
400ml (14fl oz) red wine
2 carrots, sliced
300g (10½oz) chestnut mushrooms, trimmed and sliced

TO SERVE

Braised Cabbage and Peas (*see* page 178)

TIPS

Although you can add all the raw ingredients straight to a slow cooker, the flavour of the beef will be so much better if it is browned first.

This dish is ideal for batch cooking and making ahead and it freezes well. Cool, then transfer to an airtight container and keep in the refrigerator for up to 3 days or freeze for up to 3 months. Defrost thoroughly before reheating to serve.

If oven-cooking, preheat the oven to 130°C Fan/150°C/300°F/Gas Mark 2.

Pat the ox cheeks dry with kitchen paper. Combine the flour, salt and pepper in a bowl, then add the ox cheeks and toss to coat.

Sit the garlic bulb the right way up and slice just the top off so the cloves are exposed but the bulb is intact. Set aside.

Heat a large lidded casserole pan and add the olive oil. Colour the ox cheeks on all sides on a high heat, about 5 minutes. If using shin or bavette, you may need to do this in batches. Set aside on a plate.

Add the butter and onions to the casserole pan. Colour on a medium heat for a minute, then add a splash of water to deglaze the bottom of the pan.

You can now transfer all the ingredients (including the browned ox cheeks), apart from the mushrooms, to a slow cooker (if using), nestling the garlic bulb in, cut-side up. Put a lid on and cook on low for 8 hours. Add the mushrooms for the final hour. Alternatively, they can be sautéed in a little extra olive oil or butter in a pan on a medium heat for a few minutes and added just before you serve.

For the oven method, add the rosemary, bay leaves, tomato purée, stock and red wine to the casserole pan. Return the browned ox cheeks and their juices to the pan. Nestle the garlic bulb in, cut-side up. Bring to a simmer, then cover, transfer to the oven and cook for 4 hours. An hour before the end of the cooking, add the carrots and mushrooms.

Once ready, the ox cheeks will be meltingly tender. Squeeze the garlic out of its skin into the sauce and stir in. The cheeks can be served whole, or the meat pulled apart or sliced. If using shin or bavette, pull the meat apart in the pan. Serve with Braised Cabbage and Peas.

Sometimes a bowl of peas or some steamed broccoli is just the ticket to accompany a meal. In many cases, nothing more is needed as I try to incorporate vegetables into my one-pan and one-tray meals. However, there are times when you might want something a little different to take your meal to the next level. Whether it's a Sunday roast, a one-pan family supper or a dinner party spread, I've got you covered.

Side Orders

Black Bean & Edamame Salad
Couscous Salad
Boulangère Potatoes
Maple-roasted Root Vegetables
Potato Salad
Braised Cabbage & Peas
Sautéed Broccoli
Green Beans Almondine
Pan-fried Greens
Crispy Fries
Cauliflower Cheese
Lemony Garlic Potatoes with Aioli

Prep time: 10 minutes | **Cooking time:** 2 minutes | **Serves:** 6

Black Bean & Edamame Salad

They say you eat with your eyes. This vibrant salad, packed with goodness and protein, has a Mexican vibe from chipotle paste and lime juice. You can play with the ingredients below depending on your tastes or your diners. It's delicious served with steak, chicken or fish. ***See* pages 68–9 for Black Bean & Edamame Salad photographed with Steak with Aji Verde.**

200g (7oz) edamame beans (typically sold frozen and also known as soy beans)
160g (5¾oz) sweetcorn kernels (frozen, canned or from a jar)
2 teaspoons chipotle paste
3 tablespoons olive oil
1 tablespoon honey or agave nectar
juice of 2 limes
½ teaspoon salt
400g (14oz) can black beans, drained and rinsed
200g (7oz) fresh ripe mango flesh, cubed
1 red pepper, cored, deseeded and finely chopped
2 ripe avocados, pitted, peeled and cubed
bunch of fresh coriander, leaves picked and chopped
1 red chilli, chopped (optional)
200g (7oz) fresh tomatoes, roughly chopped

If the edamame beans and sweetcorn are frozen, add them to a pan of simmering water for 2 minutes, then drain and cool.

Mix the chipotle paste, olive oil, honey or agave nectar, lime juice and salt together in a small bowl to make a dressing.

Combine all the salad ingredients in a serving bowl, toss through the dressing, and serve.

TIP

The salad will keep in an airtight container in the refrigerator for up to 3 days and it makes an excellent healthy lunch. Dress the salad just before serving.

Prep time: 10 minutes | Cooking time: 15 minutes | Serves: 6–8

Couscous Salad

Don't be put off by dry and bland couscous you may have tried in the past; this salad is packed with tangy flavour and texture. If it doesn't all get eaten in the first sitting, it'll happily sit in the refrigerator for a few days to serve for future lunches or another evening meal. *See* page 26 for Couscous Salad photographed with Stuffed Mushrooms.

2 tablespoons extra virgin olive oil, plus extra for drizzling
2 red onions, sliced
2 red peppers, cored, deseeded and chopped
2 teaspoons ras el hanout
1 tablespoon balsamic vinegar
250g (9oz) couscous
300ml (10fl oz) hot vegetable stock
400g (14oz) can chickpeas, drained and rinsed
150g (5½oz) tomatoes, chopped
½ cucumber, chopped
1 preserved lemon, chopped
handful of herb leaves, chopped (a mix of basil, parsley and mint is ideal)
60g (2¼oz) pine nuts or flaked almonds (optional)
juice of ½ lemon
salt and pepper

Add the 2 tablespoons of olive oil to a frying pan, together with the red onions and peppers. Season with salt and pepper and cook on a medium heat until softened, about 5 minutes. Stir in the ras el hanout and balsamic vinegar and cook for a further 10 minutes until caramelized. Remove from the heat and set aside.

Put the couscous in a large, heatproof serving bowl and pour over the hot stock. Give the couscous a quick stir, then cover and leave for at least 10 minutes until tender. Fork through the couscous until fluffy.

Add all the ingredients (*see* Tip) to the couscous, finishing with a squeeze of lemon and a drizzle of extra virgin olive oil. Serve.

TIP

If adding the pine nuts or flaked almonds, only do so at the end just before serving as they will go soft quite quickly. The salad can be made ahead. Store it in an airtight container in the refrigerator for up to 3 days. Stir in the pine nuts or flaked almonds (if using) just before serving.

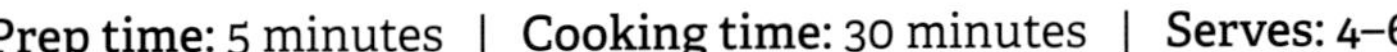

Prep time: 5 minutes | Cooking time: 30 minutes | Serves: 4–6

Boulangère Potatoes

Boulangère potatoes are one of my favourite side dishes, but the classic version of thinly sliced potatoes baked in the oven is quite a lot of effort, particularly mid-week. So I created this quicker alternative method where the whole dish is cooked on the hob in one pan. The potatoes are roughly sliced by hand and there's no need to peel them first.

1 tablespoon olive oil
15g (½oz) butter
1 onion, sliced
1kg (2lb 4oz) floury potatoes (Say King Edward or Maris Piper are ideal), sliced (approx. 1cm/½ inch thick)
pepper
500ml (18fl oz) vegetable, beef or chicken stock or bone broth
fresh thyme leaves, to garnish

Heat the butter and oil in a large pan and add the onions. Cook on a medium heat for 2 minutes before adding the potatoes and cook for 2 minutes on each side, until starting to brown. Season with pepper.

Pour over the stock or bone broth. If using bone broth, add a teaspoon of salt (not needed if using stock). Simmer for 25–30 minutes, turning the potatoes a few times during the cooking. If the dish is becoming dry, add a splash of water.

Finish with fresh thyme leaves.

TIP
Make extra and they will keep in the refrigerator for 3 days. Reheat thoroughly on the hob before serving.

Prep time: 10 minutes | **Cooking time:** 40 minutes | **Serves:** 6

Maple-roasted Root Vegetables

These are a fabulous side and they pair so well with a roasting joint or fish. You can choose from the list of root vegetables below – use them all or just stick with one. I use this recipe for carrots and parsnips all the time. *See* page 155 for Maple-roasted Root Vegetables photographed with Glazed Ham.

1kg (2lb 4oz) root vegetables – carrots, parsnips, beetroots, radishes, sweet potatoes
2 tablespoons olive oil
2 tablespoons maple syrup
1 teaspoon salt
¼ teaspoon pepper
30g (1oz) butter
1 heaped tablespoon chopped sage or rosemary leaves

Preheat the oven to 200°C Fan/220°C/425°F/ Gas Mark 7.

If using baby veg, there is normally no need to peel them. Trim and peel larger carrots or parsnips. Top and tail the beetroots. Top the turnips.

Baby carrots and parsnips can stay whole. Cut large carrots and parsnips into quarters lengthways. Cut all the other vegetables into 4cm (1½ inch) pieces.

Add the vegetables to a roasting tray and then add the olive oil, maple syrup, salt and pepper. Toss the vegetables so they are coated, then dot the butter around the vegetables.

Roast for 35 minutes, turning the veg halfway through. Use a knife to check the vegetables are cooked. Toss through the sage or rosemary and return the roasting tray to the oven for another 5 minutes, then serve.

Air fryer method: Toss the vegetables through all the remaining ingredients apart from the herbs and cook in a preheated air fryer at 200°C/400°C for 8 minutes. Toss through the herbs and cook for 4 minutes more until tender.

TIP

You can make this ahead and reheat it when ready. Cool the roasted veg, transfer to an airtight container and refrigerate for up to 3 days, then reheat before serving.

ADAPTATION

- Add some hot cooked lentils and shredded green leaves (such as spinach or kale) to the roasted veg just before serving and you have a hearty vegetarian/vegan meal.

Prep time: 10 minutes | Cooking time: 15 minutes | Serves: 6–8

Potato Salad

When I was growing up, a potato salad consisted of boiled potatoes mixed with mayonnaise, chopped egg and often raw onion. Here I've kept the potato and egg but the rest is all change! I've also provided some suggestions for embellishments, depending on tastes.

1kg (2lb 4oz) new potatoes (Jersey Royals are ideal), scrubbed
2 teaspoons salt
½ cucumber
5 tablespoons Greek yogurt (or use a dairy-free alternative)
¼ teaspoon pepper
1 garlic clove, crushed
1½ tablespoons apple cider or white wine vinegar
2 teaspoons English mustard
2 tablespoons chopped chives
2 tablespoons chopped parsley
6 spring onions, trimmed and sliced
3 celery sticks, finely sliced
2 hard-boiled eggs, shelled and chopped

OPTIONAL EXTRAS
crispy bacon (*see* Tips)
handful of radishes, thinly sliced (these add a lovely pepperiness to the salad)
50g (1¾oz) crumbled feta cheese
handful of pitted black olives

Halve or quarter the potatoes – you want them in roughly 3cm (1¼ inch) pieces.

Add the potatoes to a saucepan, cover with cold water, add 1 teaspoon of the salt and bring to the boil, then reduce the heat and simmer for 10 minutes. Check the potatoes are cooked by piercing one with a knife – it should easily skewer the middle of the potato. Drain the potatoes and leave to cool.

Cut the cucumber in half lengthways, then using a teaspoon, scrape out the seeds and discard them. Chop the cucumber into 1cm (½ inch) pieces.

Mix the yogurt, the remaining salt, the pepper, garlic, vinegar, mustard and half the herbs together in a small bowl.

Once the potatoes have cooled (they don't have to be cold but if they're too hot they will cook the yogurt), combine all the salad ingredients (including any optional extras) in a serving bowl, then add the yogurt dressing and stir together to mix. Finish with a sprinkling of the remaining herbs.

TIPS

If you clean the eggs carefully first, they can be simmered in the same water as the potatoes for 8 minutes, then cooled before shelling.

For the yogurt dressing, use a 50:50 mix of Greek yogurt to mayonnaise instead of all yogurt.

To make crispy bacon, pan-fry 200g (7oz) rindless bacon rashers in a dry frying pan on a medium heat until cooked and crispy, turning once, then cool and roughly chop.

This potato salad can be made ahead, then stored in an airtight container in the refrigerator for up to 3 days.

ADAPTATION

▸ For gluten-free, use a gluten-free mustard.

Prep time: 10 minutes | **Cooking time:** 25 minutes | **Serves:** 6–8

Braised Cabbage & Peas

This recipe converted my sons to eating cabbage. We often have this as a side dish to a roast dinner or with sausages and mashed potatoes. The crispy bacon topping is optional, or can be served separately if you need to keep the dish veggie for some. *See* page 169 for Braised Cabbage & Peas photographed with Slow-cooked Ox Cheeks in Red Wine.

1 savoy cabbage or sweetheart (hispi) cabbage
1 tablespoon olive oil
125g (4½oz) rindless smoked streaky bacon rashers, cut into thin strips (optional)
30g (1oz) butter
1 banana shallot or 1 small onion, finely chopped
1 large garlic clove, crushed
2 tablespoons sherry or red wine vinegar
300ml (10fl oz) vegetable stock
250g (9oz) frozen peas
salt and pepper

Discard the outer leaves of the cabbage and halve it. Cut out the woody core and discard. Finely slice the cabbage halves so you have ribbons of cabbage leaves.

Heat a large saucepan until hot, add the olive oil and bacon strips (if using) and cook the bacon on a medium heat until cooked and crisp, about 5 minutes. Set the bacon aside on a plate.

Add the butter to the same pan and let it melt, then add the shallot or onion and garlic. Soften on a low heat for a few minutes, then add the vinegar. After a minute, add the shredded cabbage. Give the pan a stir and then pour in the stock. Bring to a simmer, then put a lid on the pan and cook on a low heat for 10 minutes.

Add the frozen peas and stir into the cabbage mixture (tongs make the job easier), then simmer with the lid off for 5 minutes.

Stir through the crispy bacon bits (if using). Taste and check for seasoning. It will need a good few grinds of pepper but may not need any salt as the stock and bacon will be salty. Serve each portion with a spoonful of the braising juices.

TIP

You can make this whole dish ahead, then cool, cover (or transfer to an airtight container) and refrigerate for up to 3 days, then reheat when needed.

ADAPTATION

▶ For gluten-free, use a gluten-free stock cube or bouillon powder, or use homemade veg stock.

Prep time: 5 minutes | **Cooking time:** 10 minutes | **Serves:** 6–8

Sautéed Broccoli

We eat so much broccoli in our house. Typically this tasty veg is simply simmered and plopped on the side of whatever is for dinner, but sometimes you might want to switch it up. When that's the case, try this recipe.

400g (14oz) broccoli crown, trimmed and broken into florets, or Tenderstem broccoli, trimmed
1 tablespoon olive oil
2 garlic cloves, sliced
couple of pinches of chilli flakes
¼ teaspoon salt

Add the broccoli to a pan and add 100ml (3½fl oz) of water. The water is not supposed to cover the broccoli. Bring to a simmer, then put a lid on the pan and cook for 5 minutes. Drain off any water.

Add the olive oil to the pan, along with the garlic slices and chilli flakes. Stir-fry on a high heat for 2 minutes, then finish with the salt and serve.

Prep time: 5 minutes | **Cooking time:** 12 minutes | **Serves:** 6

Green Beans Almondine

This is my favourite way to dress up the humble green bean. When beans are in season, I would happily eat a plate of these beans almondine for my lunch, but they're a great side to any meat or fish dish. The buttery toasted almonds add a lovely texture contrast to the beans. ***See* page 61 for Green Beans Almondine photographed with Saltimbocca.**

400g (14oz) French green beans, topped and tailed
1 teaspoon salt
25g (1oz) butter
30g (1oz) flaked almonds
1 banana shallot or ½ small onion, finely chopped
finely grated zest of ½ lemon, plus 1 tablespoon lemon juice
ground black pepper, to serve

Put the green beans in a pan and add the measured salt. Add enough water so the beans are just covered. Bring to a simmer and cook for 5 minutes, then drain in a colander.

Return the pan to the heat. Add the butter, let it melt, then add the flaked almonds. Cook on a medium heat for 3 minutes. The almonds should start to take on some colour. Add the shallot or onion and cook for 3 more minutes.

Return the green beans to the pan, then add the lemon zest and lemon juice. Toss everything together, season with the pepper and serve.

TIP

The salt in the water not only seasons the beans, it helps to retain their vibrant colour.

ADAPTATION

▸ You can use the same recipe for Tenderstem broccoli or runner beans.

Prep time: 5 minutes | **Cooking time:** 8 minutes | **Serves:** 4

Pan-fried Greens

Asian flavours inspire a lot of my recipes, and people often ask what to serve alongside these dishes other than noodles and rice. These pan-fried greens are the answer. You can use the green veg below as a pick and choose list. Just combine what you like and what is seasonal, keeping the total quantity of veg the same. *See* page 73 for Pan-fried Greens photographed with Thai-style Fishcakes.

150g (5½oz) Tenderstem broccoli, trimmed
150g (5½oz) French green beans, topped and tailed
235g (8¼oz)/2 pak choi
150g (5½oz) asparagus spears
1 tablespoon vegetable or groundnut oil
2 teaspoons sesame oil (or sub with veg oil)
1 garlic clove, crushed
2 teaspoons grated fresh root ginger, or use ginger paste
1 red chilli, chopped (optional)
1 tablespoon soy sauce
2 tablespoons oyster sauce, or use Lee Kum Kee vegan oyster flavour or mushroom sauce

Add the Tenderstem broccoli and green beans to a pan of simmering water and cook for 3 minutes, then drain in a colander.

Meanwhile, trim the very bottom off the pak choi but so each bulb stays intact, then quarter each bulb lengthways.

Snap off the woody ends from the asparagus. Halve each asparagus spear so you have the tips and stems separate.

Heat a large, heavy-based frying pan or wok until hot, then add both oils. Add the asparagus stems and stir-fry on a high heat for a couple of minutes. Add the asparagus tips and stir-fry for a minute.

Add the garlic, ginger, chilli (if using) and the blanched French green beans and Tenderstem broccoli, along with the pak choi. Stir-fry for 2 minutes before adding the soy sauce and oyster sauce or Lee Kum Kee vegan/mushroom sauce.

Combine and then serve immediately.

Prep time: 15 minutes | **Cooking time:** 30–35 minutes | **Serves:** 4

Crispy Fries

Who doesn't love a crispy fry?! These homemade chips will be so much better and healthier than any you buy frozen. Choose whether you want to make regular or sweet potato fries. If you prefer a chunkier chip, there's an adaptation below. ***See* pages 68–9 for Crispy Fries photographed with Steak with Aji Verde and page 119 with Gyros.**

1kg (2lb 4oz) floury potatoes (King Edward or Maris Piper are ideal), or sweet potatoes
2 teaspoons salt
1 tablespoon cornflour
1 tablespoon smoked paprika (optional)
1 tablespoon garlic granules (optional)
4 tablespoons olive oil

Preheat the oven to 200°C Fan/220°C/425°F/Gas Mark 7. Line a large baking sheet with nonstick baking paper.

Slice the potatoes, stack the slices and slice again so you have matchsticks. Ideally your fries should be 6mm (¼ inch) thick.

Put the fries into a colander and rinse well with water. Shake and allow to dry for as long as possible or blot with a clean tea towel.

Add the fries to a large bowl with the salt, cornflour, smoked paprika and garlic granules (if using) and toss to coat. Add the olive oil and toss to mix again.

Arrange the fries in a single layer on the lined baking sheet and bake for 30–35 minutes, turning the fries at least once during the cooking time. You'll know when they're ready – they will look deliciously golden and crisp. Tuck in and enjoy!

Air fryer method: Cook the fries in a preheated air fryer at 190°C/375°F for 15 minutes, giving the basket a shake at least once during the cooking time. Depending on your air fryer capacity, you may need to cook the fries in two batches.

ADAPTATIONS

- For chunky chips, cut the potatoes into 1cm (½ inch) chips. Place in a saucepan, cover with water, bring to the boil and simmer for 3 minutes. Drain and allow them to steam-dry before tossing through the salt, cornflour, smoked paprika and garlic granules (if using). Add the olive oil and toss to mix again. Spread out on the lined baking sheet and bake in a preheated oven at 200°C Fan/220°C/425°F/Gas Mark 7 for 25–30 minutes, turning the chips at least once during cooking.
- In a preheated air fryer, the chunky chips will take 20 minutes at 190°C/375°F. Turn the chips at least once during the cooking time.

Prep time: 10 minutes | **Cooking time:** 40–50 minutes | **Serves:** 6–8

Cauliflower Cheese

This cauliflower cheese is like no other: creamy, slightly smoky with the mildest hint of garlic. And, of course, it's cheesy! I think the idea of making a roux, and the panic that the sauce will be lumpy, puts a lot of people off making cauli cheese. This recipe uses a 'throw-it-all-in' method for the sauce which honestly works. Cauli cheese is not just for roast dinners, it's great served with ham and chips, sausages and fish or on its own for a veggie dish.

2 cauliflowers, trimmed and broken into florets
60g (2¼oz) butter
60g (2¼oz) plain flour
600ml (20fl oz) milk
2 teaspoons smoked paprika
1 garlic clove, crushed, or 1 teaspoon garlic paste, or 1 teaspoon garlic granules
120g (4¼oz) Cheddar cheese, grated

Preheat the oven to 180°C Fan/200°C/400°F/ Gas Mark 6.

Bring a large pan of salted water to the boil, then add the cauli florets. Reduce to a simmer, cook for 5 minutes, then drain. Set aside and cool slightly.

Meanwhile, add the butter, flour, milk, smoked paprika and garlic to a separate saucepan and whisk together on a low heat. Keep whisking as the sauce heats until it is smooth and thickened, then simmer for 5 minutes, stirring every minute. Stir through three-quarters of the grated cheese, leaving the rest to sprinkle on top.

Arrange the cauliflower in an ovenproof dish. The cauliflower should not be steaming when the cheese sauce is poured on, otherwise it will run off. Pour over the sauce and sprinkle over the remaining Cheddar.

Bake for 30–40 minutes, or until the top is golden and bubbling, then serve.

Air fryer method: Cook the cauliflower cheese in a preheated air fryer at 200°C/400°F for 6 minutes until golden and bubbling.

TIPS

You can make this ahead, cool, cover and refrigerate for up to 3 days, then reheat when needed. It freezes well too – cool, transfer to an airtight container and freeze for up to 3 months (defrost before reheating to serve).

If you want to make extra cheese sauce for another meal (mac and cheese, for example), that too can be cooled and stored in an airtight container and either refrigerated for a couple of days or frozen for up to 3 months. Defrost before reheating to serve.

ADAPTATION

▶ Try adding some cooked crispy bacon pieces or cooked chopped chorizo sausage to your cauliflower cheese. Stir the cooked bacon or chorizo through the cheese sauce before pouring over the cauliflower.

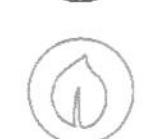

Prep time: 10 minutes | **Cooking time:** 1 hour–1 hour 10 minutes | **Serves:** 6

Lemony Garlic Potatoes with Aioli

These potatoes are so moreish. Pair them with literally anything – steaks, a roast chicken, fish... or just eat a bowl of them dipped into the aioli!

1.5kg (3lb 5oz) potatoes, left whole (no need to peel)
2 teaspoons salt
finely grated zest and juice of 1 lemon
3 garlic cloves, crushed
1 teaspoon pepper
4 tablespoons olive oil
chopped parsley or oregano, to garnish (optional)

FOR THE AIOLI
100g (3½oz) good-quality mayonnaise (avocado oil mayo is the best)
1 garlic clove, crushed, or 1½ teaspoons garlic paste
1 tablespoon lemon juice
½ teaspoon salt

Preheat the oven to 180°C Fan/200°C/400°F/Gas Mark 6. Line a baking tray with nonstick baking paper.

Add the potatoes to a saucepan and cover with water. Add 1 teaspoon of the salt and bring to the boil, then reduce the heat and simmer for 7 minutes – they should be soft but not falling apart. Drain and cool slightly.

Mix together the lemon zest and juice, garlic, the remaining salt, the pepper and olive oil in a small bowl or jug.

When the potatoes are cool enough to handle, slice them into 1.5cm (⅝ inch) discs. They should be slightly falling apart on the outside – this delivers lovely crunchy bits when they're roasted.

Tip the potatoes on to the lined baking tray. Pour over the dressing and toss gently so the potatoes are coated. Arrange in a single layer.

Roast for 50–60 minutes, turning halfway through, until golden and crispy. Finish with a sprinkling of chopped parsley or oregano.

While the potatoes are roasting, make the aioli. Simply combine all the ingredients in a small bowl.

Serve the potatoes with the aioli alongside for spooning or dipping.

Air fryer method: Cook the potatoes in a preheated air fryer at 200°C/400°F for 20–25 minutes until golden and crispy, turning them once or twice partway through.

TIP
The cooked potatoes are great for batch cooking and making ahead and can be frozen. Once cool, transfer them to an airtight container and freeze for up to 3 months. Defrost before reheating to serve.

Glossary of UK/US Terms

UK	US
aubergine	eggplant
bacon rasher	bacon slice
beetroot	beet
bicarbonate of soda	baking soda
butter beans	lima beans
celery stick	celery stalk
chestnut mushrooms	cremini mushrooms
chickpeas	garbanzo beans
chilli (fresh chillies)	chile(s)
chilli (chilli powder, chilli sauce, etc)	chili
chilli flakes	dried red pepper flakes
chopping board	cutting board
clingfilm	plastic wrap
cornflour	cornstarch
courgette	zucchini
defrost	thaw
double cream	heavy cream
flaked almonds	slivered almonds
fresh coriander	cilantro
frying pan	skillet
grill (v.)	broil
grill (n.)	broiler
heavy-based	heavy-bottomed
hob	stovetop
jug	pitcher
kitchen paper	paper towels
mangetout	snow peas
natural yogurt	plain yogurt
nonstick baking paper	parchment paper
plain flour	all-purpose flour
porridge oats	rolled oats
prawn	shrimp
rocket	arugula
self-raising flour	self-rising flour
shop-bought	store-bought
sieve	strainer
soured cream	sour cream
spring onion	scallion
store cupboard	pantry
takeaway	take out
tea towel	dish towel
tomato purée	tomato paste

Index

Acknowledgements

This book is dedicated to my late husband, Nigel. Without his support and encouragement, I would never have started Anna's Family Kitchen and made it what it is today. We started talking about the possibility of a second book while he was ill and, despite his condition deteriorating, it gave both of us something positive to focus on. After his death, I worried if I could ever find the passion and energy needed to bring this book to life, but the prospect of not doing it was unthinkable, and I felt his unwavering faith in me keenly. Writing this book gave me a sense of purpose when times were at their toughest and was a most welcome distraction to loss.

My love and gratitude go to my three children, Mia, Tom and Finn. You three are my world and my reason to put one foot in front of the other and keep cooking and creating. You are my best and most important critics.

My eternal thanks go to my dearest friends – you know who you are. You have propped me up when needed, been my sounding board on matters family related, recipe related, pet related. Without your unwavering support over the past 18 months, I don't think I would made it through. Juliette Brown, thank you for your fantastic editing skills. You are always able to put into words exactly what I am trying inelegantly to say. Thanks to Roberta Allen for your recipe testing and for being my sounding board.

I wouldn't have one cookbook, let alone two, if it wasn't for my social media family. Thank you to everyone who follows my recipes on social media, for all the support, positivity, messages and recipe shares. This wonderful community have always been so kind and supportive.

I worked with the best team on this cookbook. Huge thanks go to everyone at Octopus – Yasia Williams, Scarlet Furness and Isabel Jessop who saw my vision, took a leap of faith and made *Spinning Plates* happen. I am so grateful for your kindness, guidance and meticulous editing throughout the whole process. Thank you to my agent Clare Hulton for all your support throughout. Chris Terry, Holly Cochrane, Emma Cantlay, Caitlin Macdonald and Tamsin Weston – you really were the dream team. Your attention to detail on every part of the shoot process was second to none. I learned so much from you all and I cannot thank you enough.

About the Author

Anna Stanford is a home cook, foodie and mum to her three children. She started Anna's Family Kitchen in July 2018 and has grown a loyal community across her website, Instagram and Facebook who enjoy her minimal faff, family-friendly recipes.

Like so many parents, Anna is used to catering to multiple dietary requirements and changing preferences within her family. That's why all her recipes have easy swaps, switches and tips to make it possible to cater for the whole family with one delicious, balanced and fuss-free meal.

Spinning Plates is the eagerly anticipated follow-up to Anna's bestselling first book, *Anna's Family Kitchen*.

Website: annasfamilykitchen.com
Instagram: @annasfamilykitchen
Facebook: Anna's Family Kitchen